W0232908

PENGUIN BOOKS
THE ABSENT TRAVELLER

Arvind Krishna Mehrotra was born in Lahore in 1947. He is the author of four books of poems, the most recent of which is *The Transfiguring Places* (1998). He has edited *The Oxford India Anthology of Twelve Modern Indian Poets* (1992), *An Illustrated History of Indian Literature in English* (2003), and *The Last Bungalow: Writings on Allahabad* (2007). He lives in Allahabad and Dehra Dun.

Praise for the book

'A finely crafted jewel, scintillating and complete in itself.'
—Adil Jussawalla, *Indian Review of Books*

'Mehrotra lets the originals speak for themselves, trusting them sufficiently, without embellishing them with needless lyricism, so that the poetry seems ancient and contemporary simultaneously.'
—Agha Shahid Ali, *India Today*

'The verses in this book are imagistic, epigrammatic, lapidary, threadbare. Nothing is spelt out, but the suggestion and suggestiveness contained in them open out a whole world of feeling and passion which one can share and understand 1800 years after their first utterance.'
—Rukun Advani, *Indian Express Magazine*

'The readability and accessibility of the translation will give readers of English the same joy which may have once been the preserve of a few of Hala's Prakrit-speaking companions.'
—Jyotindra Jain, *Times of India*

'Mehrotra's translation serves to repudiate assumptions about the lack of sophistication outside the Sanskrit tradition. . . His English is clear and strong, his abrupt rhythms matching the sound quality of the Prakrit.'
—Arshia Sattar, *Debonair*

'Mehrotra's renderings have brevity, precision and clarity. . . Some very erotic poems, referring to *viparitarata*, have not been excluded.'
—Krishna Chaitanya, *The Telegraph*

'We are doubly fortunate when very good poets take time off from their own poetry to translate the work of others. Think only of Pound's exquisite translations from the Chinese or Czeslaw Milosz's of Zbigniew Herbert, and you'll see what I mean. In *The Absent Traveller*, Arvind Krishna Mehrotra, with a poet's instinct, unlocks and showcases the poetry of a time not our own. For this we cannot but be grateful.'
—David Davidar, *The Hindu*

'Adds another gem to the world of Indian poetry—a field that has all too often suffered from inadequate translations.'
—Ashok Chopra, *Hindustan Times*

'It was a revelation to me. Here was a work that dealt with real sex and love (albeit, only heterosexual) as opposed to the coyness of contemporary Indian culture and the unreal athleticism of ancient celebrations such as the *Kama Sutra* or the temples at Khajuraho.'
—Dinyar Godrej, *New Internationalist*

THE ABSENT TRAVELLER

Prākrit Love Poetry from the
Gāthāsaptaśatī of Sātavāhana Hāla

Selected and translated from the Prākrit
by
Arvind Krishna Mehrotra

RAVI
DAYAL

PENGUIN BOOKS
An imprint of Penguin Random House

PENGUIN BOOKS

USA | Canada | UK | Ireland | Australia
New Zealand | India | South Africa | China | Singapore

Penguin Books is part of the Penguin Random House group of companies
whose addresses can be found at global.penguinrandomhouse.com

Published by Penguin Random House India Pvt. Ltd
4th Floor, Capital Tower 1, MG Road,
Gurugram 122 002, Haryana, India

First published by Ravi Dayal Publisher 1991
Published by Penguin Books India and Ravi Dayal Publisher 2008

Copyright © Arvind Krishna Mehrotra 2008

All rights reserved

10 9 8 7 6 5 4 3 2

ISBN 9780143100805

Typeset in Sabon by Eleven Arts, Delhi

Printed at Manipal Technologies Limited, India

This book is sold subject to the condition that it shall not, by way of trade
or otherwise, be lent, resold, hired out, or otherwise circulated without the
publisher's prior consent in any form of binding or cover other than that in
which it is published and without a similar condition including this condition
being imposed on the subsequent purchaser.

www.penguin.co.in

This is a legitimate digitally printed version of the book and therefore might not
have certain extra finishing on the cover.

For Vandana

ACKNOWLEDGEMENTS

I am indebted to Suresh Chandra Pandey and Uday Bhan Singh Chauhan for reading with me the Prākrit poems and Sanskrit commentaries; to Arun Kolatkar for remarks on the English of the translations and the nature of translatorese; to A.K. Ramanujan for going over the manuscript, pencil in hand; to Ravi Dayal for his advice when I had to choose between alternative versions and could not decide; to Martha Ann Selby for letting me hear the English through her American ear and for agreeing to write the Afterword. If I have strayed, it has not been through lack of telling.

Some of these translations have appeared before in *Bahuvachan, The Bombay Literary Review, Debonair, The Independent* (Bombay), *Indian Horizons* and *Poetry World 2* (London).

CONTENTS

He said: Those who know aren't upto those who love;
nor those who love, to those who delight in.

Ezra Pound, *Confucian Analects*, 6.XVIII.1

But look more deeply
                    into her maneuvers,
and puzzle as we will about them
          they may mean
                    anything

William Carlos Williams, 'Classic Picture'

TRANSLATOR'S NOTE

I

As readers we sometimes feel possessive about certain authors. They are our discoveries, and write only for us. When the whole world comes to know of them, the magic of their pages is destroyed and we feel robbed. With books like the *Gāthāsaptaśatī* the opposite is true. Instead of keeping their charms, their pleasures, to ourselves, we wish to tell others about them, and the more we tell the less exhaustible they seem. To translate such a book, then, is to share the excitement of reading.

If putting a book together is a slow, deliberate process, its beginning is often the effect of fortuity. These translations from the Prākrit might never have been made had Arun Kolatkar not introduced me to the *Gāthāsaptaśatī* one afternoon in Bombay fifteen years ago. Listening to his impromptu englishings of a few poems, I wanted to read them myself, but being ignorant of Sanskrit, German and Marathi, the three languages in which the best editions of the *Gāthāsaptaśatī* are to be found, there was no way I could. If I have done so now, Hindi and English trots, several dictionaries, and a patient tutor have played no inconsiderable part.

The *Gāthāsaptaśatī*, one of the earliest anthologies of Indian poetry to have survived, was compiled by a Sātavāhana king, perhaps Hāla, around the second century CE. It is fair to assume, however, that some of its verses go back to an even earlier period, for the legendary king drew on an oral tradition that belonged to the megalithic culture of the Deccan in the first millennium BC. Unlike later Sanskrit *subhāṣita-saṃgraha-s*, which mostly dropped out of sight for several centuries before turning up again in out of the way places (the manuscript of Vidyākara's *Subhāṣitaratnakoṣa* was discovered in a Nepalese barn), this one has seldom left the educated public's consciousness.

Metaphors take longer than a few centuries to fade if they fade at all, and Kālidāsa and the classical Tamil poets of the Eight Anthologies drew on Prākrit conventions and relocated them in their own literatures. Afterwards, works of aesthetics, poetics and grammar would quote the *Gāthāsaptaśatī's* verses; its situations would be taken over by lesser writers who were, in imitation, composing their own *saptaśatī-s* till as recently as the eighteenth century; it attracted more than a dozen commentaries; and it was translated into the major Indian languages, and into German and Persian. For 2000 years these schoolmen, poets, connoisseurs and scribes kept alive a poetic tradition in which close observation is met with economy of phrase, and bare human experience with depth of understanding.

II

The *Gāthāsaptaśatī* speaks the minute you open it, and as its translator I felt that at times I did little more than repeat in another language what it said. This indicates something about the communicability of the poems, rather than about any method of translation. The script of their images is common to the race and as old: cupped hands, a pregnant woman, a man staring. Like international signs that are understood everywhere, they hardly seem to need translators.

The language of poetry, however, is not that of representation, nor does any language have a duplicate.

To hear what Prākrit poets said with the images, we have to see them not isolated from, but as a part of, the poem's body. For example, when the traveller opens his cupped hands (161) and the woman reduces the water's trickle, they say nothing yet leave nothing unexpressed. Speech in the face of desire manifests itself in a finger's tremor and the angle of a jug.

Howsoever glancing the movement or painterly the description, there is a specific narrative—not always apparent—to which it belongs. The words are about the behaviour of birds and animals—crows (205), frogs (391), sows (402)—till the *Gāthāsaptaśatī's* intrepid commentators unfreeze the image and put it in a second context: the lover is being signalled to reach the trysting place, or warned against going there; or is being told how or how not to make love. (Some of these commentatorial suggestions are given in the notes at the back of the book.) But for the most part though, the poems are straightforward enough. Their virtue is an elegant outspokenness, the naturally figurative speech of young women (43, 93, 229) and old (239, 372, 518), go-betweens (198, 199, 220, 221) and elderly confidantes (444), wives (17, 98, 583, 656, 830, 888) and mothers (508, 885, 887), bawds (56, 258) and prostitutes (274), and on rare occasions husbands (23, 52) and travellers (396). With great precision they map out the territory of love, from the coastline of the sidelong look to the fertile valleys of infidelity.

Being essentially a woman's book, a compendium of her gestures, utterances and silences, the *Gāthāsaptaśatī* gives only one side of the story. This is as it should be, since luckless man has none to tell. 'For centuries now,' wrote Rilke in *The Notebooks of Malte Laurids Brigge*, 'women have undertaken the entire task of love; they have always played

the whole dialogue, both parts. For man has only echoed
them, and badly.'

III

This translation, as I said, is a corollary of reading, but
the simplest act of reading alters what is read. The eye, as
it passes over one passage, re-reads another, and rests on a
third, authors a simultaneous text, some form of which
will stay in the mind after the page is turned.

Translations likewise edit, highlight and compensate.
Great translations go a step further; instead of compensating
for losses, they shoot to kill, and having obliterated the
original, transmigrate its soul into another language. This
is what Edward Fitzgerald (in whom 'the soul of Omar
lodged . . . around 1857' according to a Borgesian
conjecture) and Ezra Pound ('the inventor of Chinese poetry
for our time') did, and this is what makes *The Rubaiyat of
Omar Khayyam* and 'The River-Merchant's Wife: A Letter'
immortal English poems whose Oriental origins have
ceased to matter. There is to them another aspect. During
its periods of ill health, these 'exotic injections' helped put
English poetry back on its feet. The phrase is Pound's; in
fact it is used to describe the *Rubaiyat*.

My own attempt, more modest, less homicidal, is
to provide an accurate and readable version of the
Gāthāsaptaśatī. Its verses are all in the same *āryā* metre,
and if a few of my English renderings appear somewhat
longer than others, that's because they needed a different
arrangement of pauses, and not because I added anything
to them. Indeed there are occasions when I did the opposite
and compressed a verse by dropping a word or phrase.

Any number of things can set a poem off—the cry of a
bird, a rhythm in the head, a visitor, or another poem. These

mysterious prompters disappear after leaving you inside a maze of notes and revisions, and even you cannot remember who they were or whence they came. Getting out of the maze is what matters now, and you look for the exit. On reaching one you find it blocked by the very lines that, a moment ago, had pointed it out. You again begin to write your way out of the maze, and once wake up in the middle of the night. You put your trust equally in all words, whether archaic or colloquial, obscure or common, giving each one a chance to be your guide. After exhausting your word-hoard, you open a dictionary and take the reading glass out of its case. Meanwhile, the pile of worksheets is thicker than before and you are in the middle of nowhere still.

The maze of translation is in no way different, except that here you can always retrace your steps and start all over again.

Allahabad
1990

The Absent Traveller

त्रिगित्रं पाठत्र-कव्वं पढिडं सोउं त्र जे ण त्राणन्ति।
कामस्स तत्त-तन्तिं कुणन्ति ते कहेँ ण लज्जन्ति॥

Those doctors are dead to shame
    Who never sing Prākrit verse
Nor hear it
    And treat the germ of love.   2

किं रुत्रसि ओणत्र-मुही धवलात्रन्तेसु सालि-छेत्तेसु।
हरित्राल-मण्डित्र-मुही णडि व्व सण-वाडित्रा जात्रा॥

White paddy fields
    Desolate you:
Look, the hemp's still a dancer
    Ornamented with king's yellow.   9

सहि ईरिसिव्वित्र गई मा रुव्वसु तंस-वलित्र-मुह-त्रन्दं।
एत्राणँ बाल-बालुङ्कि-तन्तु-कुडिलाणँ पेम्माणं॥

Why are you crying, friend?
    That's how love is.
A cucumber tendril   10
    Its emblem.

पात्र-पडित्रस्य पइणो पुट्ठिं पुत्ते समारुहत्तम्मि।
दढ़-मण्णु-दुम्मित्राएँ वि हासो घरेणीएँ णेक्कन्तो॥

> The remorseful husband
>> Fallen at her feet

> Their little boy
>> Climbs onto his back

> And the sullen wife
>> Laughing   11

एहिइ सो वि पउत्थो त्रहं त्र कुप्पेज्ज सो वि त्रणुणेज्ज।
इत्र कस्स वि फलइ मणोरहाणँ माला पित्रत्रत्रमम्मि॥

> My traveller-husband
>> Will return

> When I see him
>> I will look cross

> And he will
>> Reconcile me:

> A woman's dreams,
>> And so seldom true.   17

अण्णा-सत्ताइँ देन्ती तह सुरए हरिस-वित्तसित्त-कवोला।
गोसे वि आेणत्त-मुही अह सेत्ति पित्तां ण सद्दहिमो॥

> At night, cheeks blushed
>> With joy, making me do
> A hundred different things,
>> And in the morning too shy
> To even look up, I don't believe
>> It's the same woman.

23

पित्त-विरहो अप्पित्त-दंसणं अ गुरुत्ताइँ दो वि दुक्खाइं।
जीएँ तुमं कारिज्जसि तीएँ णमो आहिजाईए॥

> Separated from the woman you love,
>> To sit beside one you do not is
> To double your sorrow. I honour
>> The goodness that brings you.

24

पणत्त-कुवित्ताणँ दोण्ह वि अलित्त-पसुत्ताणँ माणइल्लाणं।
णिच्चल-णिरुद्ध-णीसास-दिण्ण-कण्णाणँ को मल्लो॥

> After a quarrel,
>> The breath suppressed,
> Their ears attentive,
>> The lovers feign sleep:
> Let's see who
>> Holds out longer.

27

णिक्किव जात्रा-भीरुत्र दुहंसण णिम्ब-ईड-सारिच्छ ।
गामो गामणि-नन्दण तुज्झ कए तह वि तणुत्राइ ॥

> O village headman's
>   Cruel-
> Hen-pecked-
>   Hard-to-get-
> Insect-inside-
>   The-neem-tree-
> Son, we grow thin
>   Without you.   30

चत्तर-घरिणी पित्र-दंसणा त्र तरुणी पउत्थ-पइत्रा त्र ।
त्रसई-सत्रज्जित्रा दुग्गंत्रा त्र ण हु खण्डित्रं सीलं ॥

> Lives in main street,
>   Attractive, young, her husband away,
> A light wench her neighbour, hard up too,
>   And, unbelievably, still chaste.   36

विरहाणलो सहिज्जइ त्रासा-बन्धेण वल्लह-जणस्स ।
एक-ग्गाम-पवासो माए मरणं विसेसेइ ॥

> Mother, were he abroad
>   I'd bear the separation
> Waiting for him,
>   But to live in separate houses
> In the same village
>   Is worse than death.   43

कल्लं किर खर-हित्रत्रो पवसिहिइ पित्रो त्ति सुण्णइ जणम्मि ।
तह वड्ढ भत्रवइ णिसे जह से कल्लं वित्र ण होइ ॥

They whisper the cruel one
    Leaves at dawn:
Grow, night,
    And blot out tomorrow.   46

थोत्रं पि ण णीसरई मज्झण्णे उत्र सरीर-तल-लुक्का ।
त्रात्रव-भएण छाही वि पहित्र किं ण वीसमसि ॥

Afraid of midday heat,
    Even your shadow
Stays under your feet:
    Come into the shade, traveller.   49

सिहि-पिच्छ-लुलित्र-केसे वेवन्तोरु बिणिमीलित्रद्धच्छि ।
दर-पुरिसाइरि विसुमरि जाणसु पुरिसाणँ जं दुक्खं ॥

Hair like ruffed feathers,
    Half open eyes,
The body in tremors needing rest:
    Having played the man,
You now know how we suffer.   52

सहइ सहइ त्ति तह तेण रामित्रा सुरत्र-दुव्वित्रद्धेण।
पम्मात्र-सिरीसाई व जह से जात्राइँ अङ्घाइं॥

Does it hurt? Is this better?
   That bungler to my girl:
And like crushed sirissa flowers
   Her limbs when he'd done.   56

त्रज्ज व्वेत्र पउत्थो उज्जात्ररत्रो जणस्स त्रज्जेत्र।
त्रज्जेत्र हलिद्दा-पिञ्जराइँ गोला-णइ-तडाइं॥

He left today, and today
   His wakeful mistresses are abroad:
The banks of the Godavari
   Are yellow with turmeric today.   58

गिम्हे दवगूगि-मसि-मइलित्राइँ दीसन्ति विज्झ-सिहराइं।
त्राससु पउत्थ-वइए ण होन्ति णव-पाउसब्भाइं॥

Cheer up! The rains aren't yet.
   Those new clouds tormenting you
Are Vindhyan hilltops blackened
   By summer's forest fires.   70

जं जं सो णिज्झत्रइ ऋङ्गोत्रासं महं ऋणिमिसच्छो।
पच्छाएमि ऋ तं तं इच्छामि ऋ तेण दीसन्तं।।

> The way he stared,
>   I kept covering myself,
> Not that I wanted him
>   To look elsewhere.

73

दिढ़-मण्णु-दुम्मित्राएँ वि गहित्रो दइत्रम्मि पेच्छह इमाए।
ऋोसरइ बालुत्रा-मुट्ठि इव्व माणो सुरसुरन्तो।।

> Her anger's a fistful of sand
>   Slipping through fingers
> When she sees him.

74

ऋहंसणेण पेम्मं ऋवेइ ऋइ-दंसणेण वि ऋवेइ।
पिसुण-जण-जम्पिएण वि ऋवेइ एमेत्र वि ऋवेइ।।

> Distance destroys love,
> So does the lack of it.
>
> Gossip destroys love,
> And sometimes
>
> It takes nothing
> To destroy love.

81

सो तुज्झ कए सुन्दरि तह छीणो सुमहिलो हलित्र उत्तो।
जह से मच्छरिणीएँ वि दोच्चं जात्राएँ पडिवण्णं।।

> Beautiful one,
>> Her husband lovesick,
> The farmer's daughter-in-law has come:
>> Once jealous wife, now willing go-between.   84

अवित्रण्ह-पेक्खणिज्जेण तक्खणं मामि तेण दिट्ठेण।
सिविणत्र-पीएण व पाणिएण तण्ह व्वित्र ण फिट्टा।।

> Aunt, can a glimpse
>> Fulfil?
> Dreaming of water   93
>> Slake thirst?

रमिऊण पत्रं पि गत्रो जाहे उवऊहिउं पडिणिउत्तो।
अहत्रं पउत्थ-पइत्रा व्व तक्खणं सो पवासि व्व॥

> Lovemaking over,
>> He gets up to go
> And doesn't reach the door
>> But is back to kiss me,
> A grass-widow waiting
>> For the exile's return.   98

बहु-पुप्फ-भरोणामित्र-भूमी-गत्र-साह सुणसु विण्णत्तिं ।
गोला-तड-वित्रड-कुडङ्ग-महुत्र सणित्रं गलिज्जासु ॥

O Mahua
Blossomed
On Godavari's
Arboured bank

Shed
Your flowers
One
After
One   103

णिप्पच्छिमाइँ ऋसइ दुक्खालोत्राइँ महुत्र-पुप्फाइं ।
चीए बन्धुस्स व त्रट्टित्राइँ रुत्रई समुच्चिणइ ॥

Mournfully
As if at the pyre
Collecting
Her loved one's relics
The wanton
Picked
The last
Mahua
Blossoms   104

जो तीएँ त्रहर-रात्रो रत्तिं उव्वासित्रो पित्रत्रत्रमेण ।
सो व्वित्र दीसइ गोसे सवत्ति-णत्रणेसु संकन्तो ॥

Her underlip's redness
    He'd removed at night,
Shows up next morning
    In her co-wives' eyes.   106

गोला-ऋड-ट्ठिञं पेच्छिऊण गह-वइ-सुञं हलिञ-सोण्हा ।
ऋाढ़त्ता उत्तरिउं दुक्खुत्ताराएँ पञ्चवीए ॥

The minute she saw
   The landowner's son on the bank,
The ploughman's daughter-in-law
   Stepped into the Godavari's swirl.   107

कमलाञ्रा ण मलिञ हंसाद्धा उड्डावित्रा ण ऋ पिउच्छा ।
केणॉवि गाम-तड़ाए ऋब्भं उत्ताणञं व्वूढं ॥

The sky whelmed over
   The village tank,
And not a lotus crushed
   Nor a flamingo less.   110

गञ-गण्ड-त्थल-णिहसण-मञ-मइलीकञ-करञ्ज-साहाहिं ।
एत्तिञ कुल-हराञ्रो णाणं वाहीए पइ-मरणं ॥

Returning home
   From her father's village

And seeing ichor stains
   On *Karañja*-branches

The hunter's wife
   Knows her husband's dead   121

हासावित्रो जणो सामलीए पढ़मं पसूत्रमाणाए।
वल्लह-वाएण त्रलं मम त्ति बहुसो भणन्तीए॥

In her first labour,
    She tells her friends,
'I won't let him
    Touch me again.' They laugh.   123

रूत्रं त्रच्छीसु ठित्रं फरिसो त्रङ्गेसु जम्मित्रं कण्णे।
हित्रत्रं हित्रए णिहित्रं वित्रोइत्रं किं त्थ देव्वेण॥

His form
    In my eyes,
His touch
    In my limbs,
His words
    In my ears,
His heart
    In my heart:
Now who's
    Separated?   132

सत्रणे चिन्तामइत्रं काऊण पित्रं णिमीलित्रच्छीए।
त्रप्पाणो उपऊढ़ो पसिढिल-वलत्राहिँ बाहाहिं॥

Lying in bed,
    Eyes closed,
Remembering him,
    Then with arms
From which bangles
    Keep slipping,
Clasps herself.   133

होन्ती वि णिप्फलच्चित्र धण-रिद्धी होइ किविण-पुरसिस्स ।
गिम्हात्रव-संतत्तस्स णित्रत्र-छाहि व्व पहित्रस्स ॥

As to a traveller
    His shadow in hot summer,
So to a niggard
    His comfortless gold.   136

सुणत्र-पउरम्मि गामे हिण्डन्ती तुह कएण सा बाला ।
पासक-सारिव्व घरं घरेण कइत्रा वि खज्जिहइ ॥

Soon to be trapped
    And devoured
By street dogs,

The starling flits
    From door to door
In search of you.   138

सम-सोक्ख-दुक्ख-परिवड्ढित्राणँ कालेण रूढ़-पेम्माणं ।
मिहुणाणँ मरइ जं तं खु जित्रइ इत्ररं मुत्रं होइ ॥

Their love by long years secured,
    Sharing each other's joys and sorrows,
Of such two the first to go lives,
    It's the other dies.   142

सहित्राहिँ भणणमाणा थणए लग्गं कुसुम्भ-पुप्फं त्ति ।
मुद्ध-बहुत्रा हसिज्जइ पप्फोडन्ती णह-वत्राइं ॥

> 'A safflower!' they shouted,
>> Pointing to the nail-mark
> On her breast, and laughed
>> When she tried to brush it.   145

णिव्वुत्त-रत्रा वि वहू सुरत्र-विराम-ट्ठिइं त्रत्राणन्ती ।
त्रविरत्र-हित्रत्रा त्रणं पि किं पि त्रत्थि त्ति चिन्तेइ ॥

> Ignorant of how it ends,
>> The bride, having come,
> Looks up as if to say
>> 'Go on'.   155

उद्धच्छो पित्रइ जलं जह विरलङ्गुली चिरं पहित्रो ।
पावालित्रा वि तह तह धारं तणुत्रं पि तणुएइ ॥

> As the traveller, eyes raised,
>> Cupped hands filled with water, spreads
> His fingers and lets it run through,
>> She pouring it reduces the trickle.   161

भिच्छात्र्ररो पेच्छइ णाहि-मण्डलं सा वि तस्स मुहत्र्रन्दं।
तं चटुत्र्रं त्र्र करङ्कु दोण्ह वि कात्र्रा विलुम्पन्ति॥

While the bhikshu
  Views her navel
And she
  His handsome face,
Crows lick clean
  Both ladle and alms bowl.   162

जेण विणा ण जिविज्जइ त्र्रणुणिज्जइ सो कत्र्रावराहो वि।
पत्ते वि णत्र्रर-दाहे भण कसूस ण वल्लहो त्र्रग्गी॥

Though he's wronged me,
  I visit him:
Fires break out,
  We still light a fire.   163

वङ्कुं को पुलइज्जउ कसूस कहिज्जउ सुहं व दुक्खं वा।
केण समं व हसिज्जउ पामर-पउरे हत्र्र-ग्गामे॥

The village blighted,
  Lewd men for company,
Nobody to receive my glances,
  Share my happiness,
My grief, my laughter.   164

ऋच्छउ दाव मणहरं पित्राइ मुह-दंसणं ऋइ-महग्घं।
तग्गाम-छेत्त-सीमा वि झत्ति तिट्ठा सुहावेइ॥

Let alone her precious face,
    There's joy in a glimpse
Of her village's outskirts.   168

णिक्कम्माहिँ वि छेत्ताहिँ पामरो णेत्र वच्चए वसइं।
मुत्र-पित्र-जात्रा-सुण्णइत्र-गेह-दुक्खं परिहरन्तो॥

Day's work done,
    The sad harvestman
Idles in the field,
    Avoids returning
To a widowed hearth.   169

पउर-जुवाणो गामो महु-मासो जोत्रणं पई ठेरो।
जुण्ण-सुरा साहीणा ऋसई मा होउ किं मरउ॥

Tight lads in fields,
    A month in springtime,
A cuss for a husband,
    Liquor in the rack,
And she young, free-hearted:
    Asking her to be faithful
Is asking her to die.   197

बहुसो वि कहिज्जन्तं तुह वत्रणं मज्झ हत्थ-संदिट्ठं ।
ण सुत्रं त्ति जम्पमाणा पुणरुत्त-सत्रं कुणइ अज्जा ॥

Your message delivered,
   'What did you say?'
She asked a hundred times,
   And a hundred times I repeated it.   198

पात्रडित्र-णेह-सब्भाव-णिब्भरं तीत्र जह तुमं दिट्ठो ।
संवरण-वावडाए अरण्णो वि जणो तह व्वेत्र ॥

To keep from spiteful tongues
   Her love for you,
She looks at everyone
   With equal affection.   199

गेणृहह पलोत्रह इमं पहसित्र-वत्रणा पइस्स अप्पेइ ।
जात्रा सुत्र-पढमुब्भिण्ण-दन्त-जुत्रलङ्कित्रं बोरं ॥

With a broad smile
   Giving him a jujube berry
Marked with their son's first bite,
   'Look at this,' she said.   200

फुट्टन्तेण वि हिअएण मामि कह णिव्वरिज्जए तम्मि।
आदंसे पडिबिम्बं व्व जम्मि दुक्खं ण संकमइ॥

Aunt,
Will he ever
Know my grief?

Can image
Pierce mirror?   204

पासासङ्की काओ णेच्छइ दिण्णं पि पहिअ-घरणीए।
आणन्त-कर-अलोगलिअ-वलअ-मज्झ-ट्टिअं पिण्डं॥

Seeing the bangle
    Fall on it
And taking it for a snare,
    The crow distrusts
The morsel she puts out.   205

बहुआइ णइ-णिउञ्जे पढमुग्गआ-सील-खण्डण-विलक्खं।
उड्डेइ विहंग-उलं हा हा पक्खेहिँ व भणन्तं॥

From the river thicket
    Where it saw a girl deflowered,
The astonished flock rose
    With a shudder.   218

सच्चं भणामि बालत्र णत्थि त्रसक्कं वसन्त-मानस्स।
गन्धेण कुरवत्राणं मणं पि त्रसइत्तणं ण गत्रा॥

Not eventful spring, not even
    The fragrance of red amaranth
Has made her wanton.   219

एक्केक्कम-वइ-वेठण-विवरन्तर-दिण्ण-तरल-णत्रणाए।
तइ वोलन्ते बालत्र पञ्जर-सउणाइत्रं तीए॥

With trembling eyes,
    Like a caged bird,
From behind the picket-fence,
    She watched you go.   220

ता किं करेउ जइ तं सि तीत्र वइ-वेट्-पेल्लित्र-थणीए।
पात्रञ्जुट्टुद्ध-क्खित्त-णीसहङ्ग्ग़ीत्र वि ण दिट्ठो॥

Her breasts
    Against the gate,
She stood on her toes
    Till her feet ached:
What more
    Could she do?   221

सव्वस्सम्मि वि दड्ढे तहवि हु हित्रत्रत्रस्स णिव्वुई च्चेत्र ।
जं तेण गाम-डाहे हत्थाहत्थिं कुडो गहित्रो ॥

> The village
>   Destroyed
> The heart
>   Ecstatic
> Houses
>   Burning
> I passed him
>   The pitcher   229

तस्स त्र सोहग्ग-गुण त्रमहिला-सरिसं च साहसं मज्झ ।
जाणइ गोला-ऊरो वासा-रत्तोद्ध-रत्तो त्र ॥

> Ask the nights of rain
>   And the Godavari in spate,
> How fortunate he is
>   And unwomanly my courage.   231

ते वोलित्रा वत्रस्ससा ताण कुडङ्गाण थाणुत्रा सेसा ।
त्रम्हे वि गत्र-वत्रात्रो मूलुच्छेत्रं गत्रं पेम्मं ॥

> Our friends
>   Gone
> Shrigged trees
>   In the garden
> We too
>   Getting old
> Left with
>   The stubs of love   232

थण-जहण-णिअम्बोवरि णहरङ्का गत्त-वत्ताणं वणिअत्ताणं ।
उव्वसिअत्राणङ्ग-णिवास-मूलबन्ध व्व दीसन्ति ॥

Nail-marks
    On the breast thigh buttock
Of a woman in decline:

Ground-stones
    Of the love god's
Derelict house.   233

जस्स जहिं वित्त पढमं तिस्सा अङ्गम्मि णिवडिआ दिट्ठी ।
तस्स तहिं चेत्र ठिआ सव्वङ्गं केण वि ण दिट्ठं ॥

No eye shifts
    From where it lights:
No one's yet
    Seen all of her.   234

पइ-पुरत्रो व्वित्र णिज्जइ विच्छु-दट्ठेत्ति जार-वेज्ज हरं ।
णिउण-सही-कर-धारित्र भुत्र-जुत्रलन्दोलिणीबाला ॥

'A scorpion's bitten her,' they cried,
    And as she thrashed about,
Her shrewd friends in her husband's presence
    Rushed her to her physician-lover.   237

विक्किणइ माह-मासम्मि पामरो पाइडिं वइल्लेण ।
णिद्धूम-मुम्मुर व्वित्र सामलीत्रों थणे पडिच्छन्तो ॥

Certain he'll find
    The smokeless warmth of chaff-fire
Between his dark wife's breasts,
    The yokel in midwinter
Trades his blanket for an ox.   238

सच्चं भणामि मरणे ट्टित्रमूहि पुण्णे तडम्मि तावीए ।
त्रज्ज वि तत्थ कुड़ङ्गे णिवडइ दिट्ठी तह च्चेत्र ॥

It's no untruth:
    My death-bed's
Near the sacred waters
    Of the Tapti

And the eye
    Just as before
Roves over
    That thicket.   239

त्रन्ध-त्रर-बोर-पत्तं व माउत्रा मह पइं विलुम्पन्ति ।
ईसात्रन्ति महं वित्र छेपाहिन्तो फणो जात्रो ॥

They snatched him from me
    As a jujube berry
From a blind man's bowl,
    And are jealous still:
O mothers,
    Their very tails are forked.   240

ण्रज्ज मए गन्तव्वं घणन्धत्रारे वि तस्स सुहत्रस्स।
ण्रज्जा णिमीलित्रच्छी पत्र-परिवाडिं घरे कुणइ॥

Tonight, she says,
    In utter darkness
I must reach the tryst:
    And practises
Going round the house
    With eyes closed.   249

तह सोण्हाइ पुलइत्रो दर-वलित्रन्तद्ध-तारत्रं पहित्रो।
जह वारित्रो वि घर-सामिएण त्रोलिन्दए वसित्रो॥

Her father-in-law said no,
    Her languor yes
To the traveller asleep
    In the terrace.   254

वइ-विवर-णिग्गत्र-दलो एरण्डो साहइ व्व तरुणाणं।
एत्थ घरे हलित्र-वहू एद्दहमेत्त-त्थणी वसइ॥

Castor leaves
Jutting through a hedge
    Are to young men
A sign: here the farmer's wife
    Has big ones.   257

गत्र-कलह-कुम्भ-संनिह-घण-पीण-णिरन्तरेहिँ तुज्झेहिं ।
उस्ससिउं पि ण तीरइ किं उण गन्तुं हत्र-थणेहिं ॥

Her cursed breasts,
    Solid and cleavageless as bosses
On a calf-elephant's forehead,
    Restrict her movement,
Make even breathing a struggle.   258

अव्वो दुक्कर-त्र्आरत्र पुणो वि तन्ति करेसि गमंणस्स ॥
त्र्अज्ज वि ण होन्ति सरला वेणीत्र तरङ्गिणो चिउरा ॥

My braided hair's
    Not straight yet,
And you again speak
    Of leaving.   273

ण वि तह छेत्र-रत्र्आइँ वि हरन्ति पुणरुत्त-रात्र-रसित्र्आइं ।
जह जत्थ व तत्थ व जह व तह व सब्भाव-णेह-रमित्र्आइं ॥

Bookish lovemaking
    Is soon repetitive:
It's the improvised style
    Wins my heart.   274

रण्णाउ तणं रण्णाउ पाणित्रं सव्वत्र सत्रं-गाहं।
तह वि मत्राणँ मईणँ त्र त्रामरणन्ताईँ पेम्माइं॥

Stag and doe
　　Enter the forest
Separately looking for
　　Herbage and water,
And stay unparted
　　Till death.　　　　　　　　　　287

धावइ वित्रलित्र-धम्मिल्ल-सिचत्र-संजमण-वावड-करग्गा।
चन्दिल-भत्र-विवलात्रन्त-डिम्भ-परिमग्गिणी घरिणी॥

Scared of the barber, the child bolts,
　　With his mother in pursuit,
Her hair pushed back
　　And skirt hitched up.　　　　　291

जह जह जरा-परिणत्रो होइ पई दुग्गत्रो विरूत्रो वि।
कुल-वालित्राणँ तह तह त्रहित्रत्रं वल्लहो होइ॥

As husbands get older,
　　Poorer, uglier,
Good wives love them
　　All the more.　　　　　　　293

एसो मामि जुवाणो वारंवारेण जं ऋडत्रणात्रो ।
गिम्हे गामेक्क-वडोत्रत्रं ब किच्छेण पावन्ति ॥

As though to draw
Cool water
From the village's
Sole well
Under the banyan,
Wantons
Line-up at his door.   294

गाम-वडस्स पिउच्छा ऋावण्डु-मुहीणँ पण्डुर-च्छात्रं ।
हित्रएण समं ऋसईणँ पडइ वात्राहत्रं पत्तं ॥

The wind blows
    The banyan's
        Yellow leaves
           Fall

And with them
    The hearts
        Of yellow-faced
           Wantons   295

ऋह ऋमह ऋात्रत्रो ऋज्ज कुल-हरात्रो त्ति छेञ्छई जारं ।
सहसागत्रस्स तुरित्रं पइणो कण्ठं मिलावेइ ॥

She thrusts her lover
    Towards her husband back early:
'This man just arrived
    From my father's village.'   301

एद्दह-मेत्तम्मि जए सुन्दर-महिला-सहस्स-भरिए वि।
त्रणुहरइ णवर तिस्सा वामद्धं दाहिणद्धस्स॥

> Though the wide world's filled
>   With beautiful women,
> Her left side compares
>   Only with her right.   303

जह जह वाएइ पित्रो तह तह णच्चामि चञ्चले पेम्मे।
वल्ली वलेइ त्रड्ङं सहाव-थद्धे वि रुक्खम्मि॥

> To his tune
>   I dance:
> Rigid tree,
>   Climbing vine.   304

हत्थेसु त्र पाएसु त्र त्रङ्गुलि-गणणाइ त्रइ-गत्रा दित्रहा।
एण्हिं उण केण गणिज्जउ त्ति भणिऊ रुत्रइ मुद्धा॥

> Unable to count
>   The days of separation
> Beyond her fingers and toes,
>   The unlettered girl breaks down.   307

पित्र-दंसण-सुह-रस-मउलित्राइँ जइ से ण होन्ति णत्रणाइं।
ता केण कण्ण-रइत्रं लक्खिज्जइ कुवलत्रं तिस्सा॥

Unless something makes her
    Close her eyes,
Who'll notice the waterlilies
    Swinging from her ears?   323

चिक्खिल्ल-खुप्प-हल-मुह-कड्डण-सिढिले पइम्मि पासुत्ते।
त्रप्पत्त-मोहण-सुहा घण-समत्रं पामरी सवइ॥

Tired from ploughing
    A heavy field,
The labourer sleeps,
    While his concupiscent wife
Blasts the monsoon.   324

सूइज्जइ हेमन्तम्मि दुग्गत्रो पुप्फुत्रा-सुत्रन्थेण।
धूम-कविलेण परिविरल-तन्तुणा जुण्ण-वडएण॥

In winter, spot a down-and-out
    By his clothes:
Reddish-brown, threadbare, smelling
    Of shard-fire.   329

सूर-च्छलेण पुत्तअ कस्स तुमं अञ्जलिं पणामेसि।
हास-कडक्खुम्मिस्सा ण होन्ति देवाणं जेक्कारा॥

Worshipping the sun, my boy?
    And with a leer? a smile?   332

मुह-विज्झवित्र-पईवं णिरुद्ध-सासं ससङ्किअ्रोल्लावं।
सवह-सत्र-रक्खित्र्भोट्टं चोरित्र-रमित्रं सुहावेइ॥

Promises
    Not to bite
The underlip,

The lamp
    Puffed out,
The speech
    A whisper,
And the breath
    Confined

Make forbidden love
    Felicitous.   333

बहल-तमा हत्र-राई अञ्झ पउत्थो पई घरं सुण्णं।
तह जग्गेसु सत्रज्जित्र ण जहा अम्हे मुसिज्जामो॥

The wretched night's dark,
    My husband's just left,
The house is empty:
    Neighbour, stay awake
And save me from theft.   335

त्रण्णह ण तीरइ च्चित्र परिवड्डन्त-गरुत्रं पित्रत्रमस्स।
मरण-विणोएण विणा विरमावेउं विरह-दुक्खं॥

> The ache
>   Of separation
> Ends
>   But in death's
> Diversions.   349

जात्रो सो वि विलक्खो मए वि हसिऊण गाढमुवगूढ़ो।
पढमोसरित्रस्स णित्रंसणस्स गण्ठिं विमग्गन्तो॥

> He groped me
>   For the underwear
> That wasn't
>   There:
>
> I saw the boy's
>   Fluster
> And embraced him
>   More tightly.   351

मा वच्च पुप्फ-लाविर देवा उत्रत्रञ्जलीहिँ तूसन्ति।
गोत्रात्ररीत्र पुत्तत्र सीलुम्मूलाइँ कूलाइं॥

> To gods we can offer water,
>   Don't go picking flowers, son:
> The banks of the Godavari
>   Will ruin you.   355

अात्रण्णेइ अडत्रणा कुडङ्ग-हेट्टम्मि दिण्ण-संकेत्रा ।
अग्ग-पत्र-पेल्लित्राणं मम्मरत्रं जुण्ण-पत्ताणं ॥

The wanton in the toft
    Hears the rustle
As he tiptoes
    Over dry leaves.   365

जो सीसम्मि विइण्णो मज्झ जुत्राणेहिँ गण-वई आसी ।
तं व्वित्र एण्हिं पणमामि हत्र-जरे होहि संतुट्ठा ॥

O hideous old age,
    Be content, I've come
To worship the stone
    Men used for my pillow.   372

भण्डन्तीत्र तणाइं सोत्तुं दिण्णाइं जाइँ पहित्रस्स ।
ताइं च्चेत्र पहाए अज्जा आत्रड्ढइ रुत्रन्ती ॥

Excellent lady
    Railed at traveller
Before giving him
    Bedstraw for the night:
Weeping she picks it
    Next morning.   379

उड्डुन्त-महारम्भे थणए दट्ठूण मुद्ध-वहुआए।
ओसण्ण-कवोलाए णीससिअं पढम-घरिणीए ॥

> The firm breasts
>> Of his new wife:
> Through hollow cheeks
>> The old one sighs.   382

अवलम्वह मा सङ्कह ण इमा गह-लङ्घिआ परिब्भमइ।
अत्थक्क-गज्जिउब्भन्त-हित्थ-हिआ पहिअ-जाआ ॥

> The woman you're frightened of
>> Isn't bewitched:
> Freak thunder and her husband's absence
>> Make her frantic.   386

तड-विणिहिअग्गहत्था वारि-तरङ्गेहिं घोलिर-णिअम्वा।
सालूरी पडिबिम्वे पुरुसाअन्तिव्व पडिहाइ ॥

> Fore-legs positioned on the bank,
>> Hinders agitating in the ripples,
> A she-frog strokes her own reflection.   391

रात्र-विरुद्धं व कहं पहित्रो पहित्रस्स साहइ ससङ्कं ।
जत्तो अम्वाण दलं तत्तो दर-णिग्गत्रं किं पि ॥

In whispers,
    Like two seditionists,
A traveller
    To his companion:
'S-s-sh! The mango's
    F-l-o-r-e-s-c-e-n-t.'   396

दट्ठूण रुन्द-तुण्डग्ग-णिग्गत्रं णित्र-सुत्रस्स दाढग्गं ।
भोण्डी विणा वि कज्जेण गाम-णित्रडे जवे चरइ ॥

The sow upon sight of her son's
    Great snout and tusks,
Needlessly roots in the barley field
    Near the village.   402

सुप्पउ तइत्रो वि गत्रो जामोत्ति सहीत्रो कीस मं भणह ।
सेहालित्राणं गन्धो ण देइ सोतुं सुत्रह तुम्हे ॥

'The third watch is ending,
    Now go to sleep.'

'O friends, the night jasmine's fragrance
    Won't let me.'   412

सुक्खन्त-बहल-कद्दम-घम्म-विसूरन्त-कमठ-पाठीणं।
दिट्ठं अदिट्ठ-उव्वं कालेण तलं तड़ाअस्स॥

> Time's at last gained
>   The bottom of the lake:
> Tortoise and catfish
>   Boil in the ooze.   414

चोरित्त-रत्त-सद्धालुइ मा पुत्ति ब्भमसु अन्धआरम्मि।
अहिआआरं लक्खिज्जसि तम-भरिए दीव-सीहव्व॥

> Careful, girl.
>   Stealing away
> Into the night
>   For the tryst,
> Looking brighter
>   Than a flame.   415

आम असइम्ह आेसर पइ-व्वए ण तुह मइलित्तं गोत्तं।
किं उण जणस्स जाअव्व चन्दिलं ता ण कामेमो॥

> We're trugs all right
>   And you're a paragon,
> But at least we don't
>   Fantasize chiropodists.   417

बालत्र तुमइ दिण्णं कण्णे काऊण बोर-संघाडिं।
लज्जालुइणी वि वहू घरं गत्रा गाम-रच्छाए॥

The jujube berry you gave her
    She stuck in her ear
And swaggered down main street.   419

चावो सहाव-सरलं विच्छिवइ सरं गुणम्मि वि पडन्तं।
वङ्कस्स उज्जुअस्स अ संबन्धो किं चिरं होइ॥

The moment it meets a bowstring,
    The simple arrow's in flight:
Can the straight be friends
    With the bent?   424

तुङ्गाणं विसेस-णिरन्तराणं [सरस]-वण-लद्ध-सोहाणं।
कत्र-कज्जाणं भडाणं व थणाणं पडणं वि रमणिज्जं॥

Like two noble warriors
    Laid low in close combat,
Your breasts even fallen
    Look handsome.   427

पुसइ खणं धुवइ खणं पप्फोडइ तक्खणं त्रत्राणन्ती।
मुद्ध-वहू थण-वट्टे दिण्णं दइएण णहर-वत्रं॥

'What's this?' she innocently wonders,
    And now washes, now rubs, now scratches
The nail-mark on her breast.   433

वासारत्ते उण्णत्र-पत्रोहरे जोव्वणे व्व वोलीणे।
पढमेक्क-कास-कुसुमं दीसइ पलित्रं व धरणीए॥

The rains end

High clouds
    (Like young breasts)
Are blown away

Like a strand of white hair
    On earth's ageing head
The first *káns* flower appears   434

सेउल्लित्र-सव्वङ्गी गोत्त-ग्गहणेण तस्स सुहत्रसस्स।
दूइं पट्ठाएन्ती तस्सेत्र घरङ्गणं पत्ता॥

His very name
    Covers her in sweat:
She dispatches the go-between,
    Then herself reaches his courtyard.   440

णित्र-वक्खारोवित्र-देह-भार-णिउणं रसं लिहन्तेण ।
वित्रसाविऊण पिज्जइ मालइ-कलित्रा महुअ्रेण ॥

The deft bee,
   His weight held back,
Endues the bud and sucks
    The white jasmine's nectar.   442

जाव ण कोस-विकासं पावइ ईसीस मालई-कलित्रा ।
मत्र्ररन्द-पाण-लोहिल्ल भमर तावच्चित्र मलेसि ॥

Before the white jasmine
   Could unfold, impetuous bee,
You'd mangled it.   444

सहि साहसु सब्भावेण पुच्छिमो किं अ्रसेस-महिलाणं ।
वड्ढन्ति कर-ठित्रा व्वित्र वलत्रा दइए पउट्ठम्मि ॥

Friend, I'm worried.
   My bangles expand
When he's abroad.
    Is this common?   453

कारिममाणन्दवडं भामिज्जन्तं बहूत्र सहित्राहिं।
पेच्छइ कुमारी-जारो हासुम्मिस्सेहिँ त्रच्छीहिं॥

> Much to her lover's amusement,
> > Her friends display the wedding-sheet.   457

सणित्रं सणित्रं ललित्रङु लीत्र मत्रण-वड-लात्रण-मिसेण।
बन्धेइ धवल-वण-वट्टत्रं व वणित्राहरे तरुणी॥

> With delicate fingers,
> > As if tying a white bandage,
> She slowly spread
> > Beeswax on sore lip.   458

रइ-विरम-लज्जित्रात्रो त्रप्पत्त-णित्रंसणात्रौँ सहस व्व।
ढक्कन्ति पित्रत्रमालिङ्गणेण जहणं कुल-बहूत्रो॥

> Petticoat misplaced,
> > The gentle woman
> Covers her thighs
> > In her husband's embrace.   459

पात्रडित्रं सोहग्गं तम्बाए उत्रह गोट्ठ-मज्झम्मि ।
दुट्ठ-वसहस्स सिङ्गे त्रक्खि-उडं कण्डुत्रन्तीए ॥

The herd saw who was favoured
     When the brown cow rubbed
Her eye on the rogue bull's horn.   460

उह खंभम-विक्खिखं रमित्रव्वत्र-लेहलाएँ त्रसईए ।
णवरङ्गत्रं कुडङ्गे धत्रं व दिण्ण त्रविणत्रस्स ॥

Look, the wanton
     Throwing off her red skirt,
Hoists immodesty's
     Flag in the park.   461

दे सुत्रणु पसित्र एण्हिं पुणो वि सुलहाइँ रूसित्रव्वाइं ।
एसा मत्रच्छि मत्र-लाञ्छणुज्जला गलइ छण-राई ॥

For our quarrels
     Let's appoint another night:
The bright one slips by.   466

के उव्वरिञ्आ के इह ण खण्डिञ्आ के ण लुत्त-गुरू-विहवा ।
णहराइं वेसिणिञ्ओ गणणा-रेहा उववहन्ति ॥

Who's spared?
Who's escaped defoul?
Who's not been gulled?

Nail-marks
On whores' bodies
Tell everything.   474

उज्जुञ्आ-रए ण तूसइ वक्कम्मि वि ञ्आञ्रमं वित्रप्पेइ ।
एत्थ ञ्अहव्वाएँ मए पिए पिञ्रं कहँ णु काञ्रव्वं ॥

He finds the missionary position
    Tiresome, and grows suspicious
If I suggest another:
    Friend, what's the way out?   476

ण वि तह ञ्अइ-गरुएण वि तम्मइ हिञ्रए भरेण गब्भसूस ।
जह विपरीञ्र-णिहुञ्रणं पिञ्रम्मि सोण्हा ञ्रपाबन्ती ॥

In the last weeks
    Of pregnancy

She's distressed by
    Her inability

To mount him   483

ञइ-कोवणा वि सासू रुत्राविञा गत्र-वईञ सोण्हाए।
पात्र-पडणोण्णत्राए दोसु वि गलिएसु वलएसु॥

When she bends to touch
    Her mother-in-law's feet
And two bangles slip
    From her thin hands, tears
Come to the cold woman's eyes.   493

खेमं कन्तो खेमं जो सो खुज्जम्बत्रो घर-दारे।
तस्स किल मत्थत्राञो को वि ञणत्थो समुप्पण्णो॥

How am I? Can't you see?
    Evil crowns the prodigious
Mango in the yard.   499

सूई-वेहे मुसलं विच्छुहमाणेण दइढलोएण।
एक्क-ग्गामे वि पित्रो समत्रं ञच्छीहिँ वि ण दिट्ठो॥

Because the jealous world must drive
    A pestle through a pinhole,
My eyes can never dwell
    On him, though he lives in my village.   502

वाउद्धत्त्र-सिचय-विहावित्रोरु-दिट्ठेण दन्त-मग्गेण।
वहु-मात्रा तोसिज्जइ णिहाण-कलसस्स व मुहेण॥

> As though she's glimpsed
> The mouth of a buried
>   Pot of gold,
>
> Her joy on seeing
> Under her daughter's
>   Wind-blown skirt
>
> A tooth-mark
>   Near the crotch.   508

सन्तमसन्तं दुक्खं सुहं च जात्त्रो घरस्स जाणन्ति।
ता पुत्तत्र महिलात्त्रो सेसात्त्रों जरा मणुस्साणं॥

> She who apprehends
>   A household's missing joy
> And present grief is a woman, son:
>   The rest a man's old age.   513

ता त्र जुत्त्राणा ता गाम-संपत्त्रा तं च अम्ह तारुणणं।
त्रक्खाणत्रं व लोत्त्रो कहेइ त्रम्हे वि तं सुणिमो॥

> Those men,
>   This once rich village,
> And days of my youth
>
> Are now stories
>   That sometimes
> Reach my ears, too.   518

णील-पड-पाउत्रझ्झी त्ति मा हु णं परिहरिज्जासु।
पट्टंसुत्रं पि णद्धं रत्रम्मि त्रवणिज्जइ च्चेत्र ॥

Don't let fustian
    Dishearten you:
Dalliance unties
    Even silk knots.   521

लज्जा चत्ता सीलं त्र खण्डित्रं त्रजस-घोसणा दिण्णा।
जस्स कए णं पित्र-सहि सो च्चेत्र जणो जणो जात्रो ॥

He, for whom I forsook
    Shame, chastity, honour,
Now sees me as just
    Another woman.   525

हसित्रं त्रटिट्ठ-दंतं भमित्रमणिक्कन्त-देहली-देसं।
दिट्ठमणुक्खित्त-मुहं एसो मग्गो कुल-वहूणं ॥

They laugh
But don't show their teeth

Travel
But don't cross the threshold

Observe
Without looking up

Twice-born women!   526

त्र्राारुहइ जुण्णत्रं खुज्जत्रं वि जं उत्र्राह वल्लरी तउसी।
णीलुप्पल्ल-परिमल-वासित्र्रसस सरत्र्रसस सो दोसो॥

If you see a colocynth
   Entwine a gnarl,
Put it to autumn's fragrance.   535

दइत्र्र-कर-ग्ग्रह-लुलित्र्रो धम्मिल्लो सीहु-गन्धित्रं वत्र्रणं।
मत्र्रणम्मि एत्तित्रं चित्र्र पसाहणं हरइ तरुणीणं॥

Liquor on their breath
   And hair tousled by lovers
Is enough to make young girls
   Fatal.   545

त्र्राालोत्र्रन्त दिसात्र्रो ससन्त जम्भन्त गन्त रोत्र्रन्त।
मुच्छन्त पडन्त खलन्त पहित्र्र किं ते पउत्थेण॥

Looking restless,
   Breathing heavily,
Yawning, humming,
   Weeping, fainting,
Falling, mammering:
   O traveller,
You'd better not go.   547

दट्ठूण तरुण-सुरअं विविह-विलासेहिँ करण-सोहिल्लं।
दीत्रो वि तग्गत्त-मणो गत्तं पि तेल्लं ण लक्खेइ॥

The lamp-oil finished,
    The wick still burns,
Engrossed in the young couple's
    Copulation.   548

वोड-सुणत्रो वित्त्रण्णो त्रत्ता मत्ता पई वि त्रण्णत्थो।
फलित्रं व मोडित्रं महिसएण को तस्स साहेउ॥

The watchdog dead,
    Mother-in-law bedridden,
My husband out of town,
    And I've no one to inform him
A buffalo ravaged the cotton last night.   550

गिरि-सोत्तो त्ति भुत्रंगं महिसो जीहइ लिहइ संतत्तो।
महिसस्स कण्ह-वत्थर-झरो त्ति सप्पो पित्रइ लालं॥

'This must be
    A mountain stream'
Thought the buffalo
    Drooling over a snake
In fierce summer heat.

'I've reached
    Black Rock Falls'
Thought the snake
    Drinking up the slabber.   552

पिसुणेन्ति कामिणीणं जल-लुक्क-पित्राावऊहण-सुहेल्लि ।
वण्डइत्र-कपोलुप्फुल्ल-णिच्चलच्छीईँ वत्राणाइं ।।

> They've embraced
>> Underwater,
> And her eyes
>> Make no secret of it.   559

धारा-धुव्वन्त-मुहा लम्बित्रा-वक्खा णिउञ्चित्रा-ग्गीवा ।
वइ-वेढ़णेसु कात्राा सूलाहिण्णा व्व दीसन्ति ॥

> Wings hanging down, necks drawn in,
>> Sitting on fences as though spitted,
> Crows get soaked in the rain.   564

त्राइ दित्रार किं ण पेच्छसि त्राात्राासं किं मुहा पलोएसि ।
जात्रााइ बाहु-मूलम्मि त्राद्ध-अन्दाण परिवाडिं ॥

> Ah, brother-in-law, turn away
>> From the night sky:
> Rows of crescent moons
>> Rise in your wife's armpits.   571

णित्र-धणित्रं उवऊहसु कुक्कुड-सद्देण झत्ति पडिबुद्ध।
पर-वसइ-वास-सङ्किर णित्रए वि घरम्मि मा भासु॥

> The cock crows and you
> > Wake up with a start:
> But you spent the night
> > In your own bed, husband.   583

खर-पवण-रत्र-गलत्थित्र-गिरिऊडावडण-भिण्ण-देहस्स।
धुक्काधुक्कइ जीत्रं व विज्जुत्रा काल-मेहस्स॥

> Lightning still throbs inside
> > The black cloud the gale
> Scruffed with electric speed
> > And flung down the mountain.   584

एक्क च्चित्र रूत्र-गुणं गामणि-धूत्रा समुव्वहइ।
त्रणिमिस-णत्रणो सत्रलो जीए देवी-कत्रो गामो॥

> The headman's pretty daughter
> > Has turned the whole village
> Into an unblinking god.   593

मालारीए वेल्लहल-बाहु-मूलावलोञ्चण-सञ्चणूहो ।
ञ्चलिञं पि भमइ कुसुमग्घ-पुच्छिरो पंसुल-जुञ्चाणो ॥

All he wants
    Is see her armpit,
So asks the garland-maker
    The price of a string.   599

गेहं व वित्त-रहिञं णिज्झर-कुहरं व सलिल-सुण्णविञं ।
गो-हण-रहिञं गोट्ठं व तीञ्च वञ्चणं तुह विञ्चोए ॥

Away from you, her face
    Is a hovel,
A dry spring's hollow,
    An empty cowshed.   611

जं तणुञ्चाञ्चइ सा तह कएण किं जेण पुच्छसि हसन्तो ।
ञ्चह गिम्हे मह पञ्चई एव्वं भणिऊण ञ्चोरुण्णा ॥

'Stop laughing, what have you
    Got to do with anorexia?
I go through this every summer,'
    She says between tears.   613

वण्ण-क्कम-रहिअस्स वि एस गुणो णवरि चित्त-कम्मस्स।
णिमिसं पि जं ण मुच्चइ पित्रो जणो गाढमुवऊढो॥

Unaided by colour,
    Mere line locks them
In deep embrace.   614

एक्कल्ल-मत्रो दिट्ठीत्र मइत्र तह पुलइत्रो सत्रणहाए।
पित्र-जात्रस्स जह धणुं पडित्रं वाहस्स हत्थात्रो॥

Deerslayer
    Aiming at doe.

Doe's eyes
    Fixed on a stag.

Deerslayer
    Discovers his wife.

Deerslayer's bow
    Drops.   620

वाउलित्रा-परिसोसण कुड़ङ्ग-पत्तलण सुलह-संकेत्र।
सोहग्ग-कणक-कस-वट्ट गिम्ह मा कह वि झिज्जिहिसि॥

Bless you, summer,
    For the perfect tryst-place:
A small dry pond,
    By green trees surrounded.   628

ऋण्णेसु पहित्र पुच्छसु वाहत्र-पुत्तेसु पुसित्र-चम्माइं।
ऋम्हँ वाह-जुत्राणो हरिणेसु धणुं ण णामेइ ॥

> Ask next door
>   For deerskins, traveller:
> Our men don't stalk
>   Blameless creatures.   631

गत्र-वहु-वेहव्वत्ररो पुत्तो मे एक्क-कण्ड-विणिवाई।
तह सोण्हाइ पुलइत्रो जह कण्ड-करण्डत्रैं वहइ ॥

> Till my daughter-in-law came,
>   My son who now lugs a quiver
> Widowed a cow-elephant
>   With a single arrow.   632

महु-मच्छित्राइ दट्ठं दट्ठूण मुहं पित्रस्स सूणोट्ठं।
ईसालुई पुलिन्दी रुक्खच्छात्रं गत्रा ऋणणं ॥

> The Pulinda's jealous wife
>   Found his lip swollen,
> And not knowing he'd been stung
>   Moved into the next tree's shade.   636

त्रलित्र-पसुत्त-वलन्तम्मि णव-वरे णव-वहूत्र वेवन्तो ।
संवेल्लित्रोरु-संजमित्र-वत्थ-गण्ठि गत्रो हत्थो ॥

As the bridegroom
    Feigning sleep
Sidles towards her,
    Her thighs stiffen and swiftly
With trembling hand
    She clasps the knot.   648

तत्तो च्चिव्र होन्ति कहा वित्रसन्ति तहिं तहिं समप्पन्ति ।
किं मण्णे माउच्छा एक्क-जुत्राणो इमो गामो ॥

He's the beginning,
    Middle, and end
Of every conversation:
    Aunt, is this
A one-man village?   650

विवरीत्र-सुरत्र-लेहल पुच्छसि मह कीस गब्भ-संभूइं ।
त्रोत्रत्ते कुम्भ-मुहे जल-लव-कणित्रा वि किं ठाइ ॥

Always wanting me
    To come on top
And complaining
    We're childless,
As if you could brim
    An inverted water-jug.   656

भर-णमित्र-णील-साहग्ग-खलित्र-चलणद्ध-विहुत्र-वक्ख-उडा।
तरु-सिहरेसु विहंगा कह कह वि लहन्ति संठाणं॥

> Wet twigs bend under the weight,
>> Feet slip and wings flap
> As birds alight on the tree's crest.　　　662

खाणेण त्र पाणेण त्र तह गहित्रो मण्डलो त्रडत्रणाए।
जह जारं त्रहिणन्दइ भुक्कइ घर-सामिए एन्ते॥

> After much training,
>> The hussy's mongrel
> Licks her lover's hand
>> And flies at her husband.　　　664

एत्थ णिमज्जइ त्रत्ता एत्थ त्रहं एत्थ परित्रणो सत्रलो।
पन्थित्र रत्ति-त्रन्धत्र मा मह सत्रणे णिमज्जिहिसि॥

> That
>> Is mother-in-law's bed
>
> My bed
>> Is here
>
> And those
>> Are the servants':
>
> Don't trip over mine,
>> Night-blind traveller.　　　669

परित्रोस-सुन्दराइं सुरएसु लहन्ति जाइँ सोक्खाइं ।
ताइं च्चित्र उण विरहे खाउग्गिण्णाइँ कीरन्ति ॥

Lovers' separation
　　Makes what once
Was pleasure
　　Seem like vomit.   670

त्रइ-दीहराइँ बहुए सीसे दीसन्ति वंस-वत्ताइं ।
भणिए भणामि त्रत्ता तुम्हाणँ वि पण्डुरा पुट्ठी ॥

Mother-in-law, one word
　　About the long bamboo leaves
In my hair, and I'll bring up
　　The dirt-marks on your back.   676

उत्र सिन्धव-पव्वत्र-सच्छहाइँ धुत्र-तूल-पुञ्ज-सरिसाइं ।
सोहन्ति सुत्रणु मुक्कोत्रत्राइँ सरए सित्रबब्भाइं ॥

White rainless
　　October clouds:
Hills of rock-salt,
　　Bins of combed cotton.   681

त्राउच्छन्ति सिरेहिँ विवलिएहिँ उत्र खडिएहिँ णिज्जन्ता।
णिप्पच्छिम-वलित्र-पलोइएहिँ महिसा कुडङ्काइं॥

Buffaloes look back
    And say goodbye to the grove,
As butchers, long knives in hand,
    Lead them away.   682

मज्झे पत्रणुत्र-पङ्कं त्रवहो-वासेसु साण-चिक्खिल्लं।
गामस्स सीस-सीमन्तत्रं व रच्छा-मुहं जात्रं॥

The rut-way
    Through the village:
Like a parting
    In its hair.   684

मा वच्चह वीसम्भं इमाणँ बहु-चाडु-कम्म-णिउणाणं।
णिव्वत्तित्र-कज्ज-परम्मुहाणँ सुणत्राणँ व खलाणं॥

Ass-sniffer one day
    And a slink the next,
Who taught the cur-dog
    His ways, brother-in-law?   688

दित्रहे दित्रहे सूसइ संकेत्रत्रत्र-भङ्क्-वड्ढित्रासङ्का ।
त्रावण्डुरोणत्र-मुही कलमेण समं कलम-गोवी ॥

Little by little
    The paddy dries:
And the pale scarecrow with it,
    Losing the tryst-place.   693

दट्ठूण हरित्र-दीहं गोसे णइ-जूरइ हलित्रो ।
त्रसई-रहस्स-मग्गं तुसार-धवले तिल-च्छेत्ते ॥

Early dawn;
His sesame field
White with dew;

A wanton's long
Green secret route
Across it;

And the ploughman
Showing no
Resentment.   695

संकोल्लित्रो व्व णिज्जइ खण्डं खण्डं कत्रो व्व पीत्रो व्व ।
वासागमम्मि मग्गो घर-हुत्रो-सु (मु) हेण पहिएण ॥

The monsoon about to break,
    Travellers hasten towards home,
Shortening, dividing, gulping
    The miles.   696

चोराणँ कामुत्राणँ अ पामर-पहित्राणँ कुक्कुडो वत्रइ।
रे रमह वहह वाहत्रह एत्थ तणुत्रात्रए रत्रणी।।

To bandits
        Lovers
Travellers
        The cock cries:

Loot
        Copulate
Speed well
        The night flies.   701

गामारुह म्हि, गामे वसामि, णत्रररट्टिइं ण त्राणामि।
णात्रररित्राणं पइणो' हरेमि, जा होमि सा होमि।।

Village-born,
        Among rustics raised,
To towns unused,
        To city-men attractive:
I am what I am.   705

रणरणत्रसुण्णहित्रत्रो चिन्तन्तो विरहदुव्वलं जात्रं।
त्रमुणित्रणित्रवसही सो वोलीणो गाममज्झेण।।

Preoccupied with thoughts
        Of his desolate wife,
The absent traveller
        Now approaches his village,
Now leaves it behind.   707

सो वि जुत्रा माणहणो, तुमं पि माणस्स त्रसहणा, पुत्ति!
मत्तच्छलेण गम्मउ सुराइ उवरिं पुससु हत्थं ॥

One proud, the other wilful:
      Act drunk, stumble, touch his hand.   715

जइ तेण तुज्झ वत्रणं ण कत्रं, मह कारणेण त्र, हत्रासे।
सा कीस खण्डित्रतडं णित्राहरं, दूइ! दुम्मेसि ॥

He's still annoyed with me,
      Oh, he refused even to meet you,
No wonder, wretch,
      Your underlip's bleeding.   718

सेउल्लणित्रंवालग्गसण्हसिचत्रस्स मग्गमलहन्तो।
सहि! मोहघोलिरो त्रज्ज तस्स हसित्रो मए हत्थो ॥

Friend, you should've seen
      His hand fumbling inside
The thin skirt glued
      To my wet fanny.   723

दूईकज्जात्रण्णणपडिरोहं मा करेहिइ इमं ति ।
उत्थंघेइ व तुरित्रं तिस्सा कण्णुप्पलं पुलत्रो ॥

> Goose pimples instantly
>> Lift the flower in her ear
> So it doesn't obstruct
>> The go-between's words.   724

गजंति घणा, पंथाणो वहुतणा त्र, पसारित्रा सरित्रा ।
त्रज्ज वि उज्जुत्रसीले ! पइणो मग्गं पलोएसि ॥

> Thunderclouds in the sky,
>> Paths overgrown, streams in flood,
> And you, innocent one, in the window,
>> Expecting him.   729

गत्र-गंडत्र-गवत्र-सरभ-सेरिह-सद्दूल-रिक्खजाईणं ।
थणत्रा वाहवहूए त्रभत्रं दाउं व णिक्कंता ॥

> The hunter's bride
>> Puts forth her breasts
> As though to sanctuary
>> Elephant and rhino,
> Blue bull and lion,
>> Buffalo, panther, and bear.   742

जं केत्रवेण पेम्मं, जं च वला, जं च त्रत्थलोहेण।
जं उवरोहणिमित्तं, णमो णमो तस्स पेम्मस्स॥

> I greet them all:
>> Love born of deceit,
> Love born of coercion,
>> Love born of cupidity,
> Love born of impediment.   744

कस्स ण सद्धा गरुत्रत्तणम्मि पइणो पसात्रमाणस्स।
जइ माणभञ्जणीत्र्रो ण होन्ति हेमन्तराईत्र्रो॥

> It's
>> Winter nights
> Make me
>> Give up pride.   745

त्रव्वो तहिं तहिं चित्र गत्रणे भमिऊण वीसमन्तेण।
वोहित्तवात्रसेण व्व हासित्र्रा दड्ढपेम्मेण॥

> Like a tired crow
>> After long wandering,
> Cursed love has returned
>> To the sea-boat it left.   746

पेम्मुम्मइयाइ मए उवऊढो हलित्रउत्तबुद्धीए।
फंसेमि जाव, फरुसो तणपुरिसो गामसीमाए॥

> Love-crazed, I embraced
> > The ploughman's son,
> Clutching on the village's border
> > A straw-man in my arms.

751

डाहेऊण सयलरणं त्रग्गी समविषमलंघणुव्वायो।
तडलंबंततणेहिं तिसिय व्व णइं समोसरइ॥

> After the conflagration,
> > Fire fled across odd ground;
> Then exhausted, on tall grass leaning,
> > Crept towards the river
> As one parched with thirst.

758

तिसिया पियउ त्ति मत्रो, मत्रो वि तिसियो मई करेऊण।
इय मयमिहुणं तिसियं पियइ ण सलिलं सिणेहेण॥

> Standing
> > Near water
> And thirsty,

> The stag
> > Wants the doe
> To drink first,

> The doe
> > The stag.

763

जह लंघेसि परवइं निययवइं भरसहं पि मोत्तूणं।
तह मण्णे, कोहलिए! त्रज्जं कल्लं पि फुट्टिहिसि॥

O pumpkin-vine,
　　Leaving your own firm trail,
You get up another,
　　And will soon come to grief.   768

त्रणुसोयइ हलियबहू रइकिररणोलुग्गपंडुरच्छायं।
रण्णंदुरदंतुक्खुत्तविसमवलियं तिलच्छेत्तं॥

In first light,
　　The ploughman's wife
Considers the bright sesame field
　　Attacking rats have laid waste.   769

त्रोवालत्रम्मि सी त्रालुत्राण वइमूलमुल्लिहंताणं।
डिंभाण कलिंचयवावडाण सुण्णो जलइ त्रग्गी॥

While shivering children
　　Rush about for fuel,
Their thorn-fire burns
　　Alone in the wood.   770

बहुएहिं जंपिएहिं सिट्ठं अम्ह सवहे करेऊण।
सद्दो च्चिय से भद्दो भोइणिजंते रसो णत्थि॥

> Her workers swear
>> The old sugar press
> Though it creaks a lot
>> Doesn't ooze much juice.   776

ण वि तह दूमेइ मणं गयस्स बन्धो वि करिणि विरहो वि।
दाणवित्रोयविमुहिए जह भमरउले भमन्तम्मि॥

> The elephant's distress
>> Isn't widowhood or captivity,
> But disappointed bees
>> Come for sweet ichor.   792

अंतो णिभुत्रट्टित्रपरित्रणाइ त्रोरुद्धदारणत्रणाइ।
गिम्हे घोरट्टुघग्घररवेण घोरंति वं घराइं॥

> In summer, behind doors
>> Shut like eyelids,
> The village at siesta; somewhere
>> A hand-mill rumbles,
> As if the houses snored.   800

कम्पासं कुप्पासन्तरम्मि तइ खित्तमिति भणिऊण।
अत्ता! वलाहिरेणं थणाण मह कारित्रावत्था॥

Mother-in-law,
    Look what he did:
Forced his hand inside my blouse,
    Said I'd stolen his cotton.   811

गाहाण अ गेत्राण अ तंतीसद्दाण पोढमहिलाण।
ताणं हो च्चित्र दण्डो, ते ताण रसं ण आणंति॥

Gāthās, songs, lute music, and
    A middlemost woman:
Some have never relished them,
    And *that* is their punishment.   815

अव्वो! ण आमि छेत्तं खज्जउ खाली वि कीरणिवहेहिं।
जाणन्ता अवि पहित्रा पुच्छन्ति पुणी पुणो मग्गं॥

Let parrots take the paddy,
    I'm not going there again:
Travellers who know the way
    Keep asking for directions.   821

कइत्रा जात्रा? कइत्रा णु सिक्खित्रा, माइत्रा! हत्रकुमारी?
तं तं जाणइ सव्वं, जं जं महिलात्रों जाणन्ति ॥

> O mother, when was she born?
> > Where did she school?
> Every art we know
> > This chit does. 825

मह पइणा थणजुत्रले पत्तं लिहित्रं ति गव्वित्रा कीस!।
त्रालिहइ महं पि पित्रो जइ से कंपो च्चित्र ण होइ ॥

> Proud, aren't you, to display
> > The beauty streaks
> Your husband's painted on your breasts?
>
> When I stood before mine,
> > His hand lost all
> Control over the line. 830

दूई ण एइ, चंदो वि उग्गत्रो, जामिणी वि बोलेइ।
सव्वं सव्वत्तो च्चित्र विसंठुलं, कस्स किं भणिमो? ॥

> The go-between's not back,
> > The moon's risen,
> Night passes, everything's amiss,
> > And no one to confide in. 854

पइणा वण्णिज्जन्ते ऋक्खाणऋसुन्दरीएँ रूवम्मि।
ईसामच्छरगरुऋं घरिणी हुंकारऋं देइ॥

Jealous of the beautiful princess,
  The wife listening to the fairy tale
Grunts 'Hmm, hmm'.   868

वाणीरकुडुंगुड्डीणसउणिकोलाहलं सुणंतीए।
घरकम्ममवावुडाए बहूए सीऋन्ति ऋंगाइं॥

When she heard the birds' flutter
  As they rose from the rattan grove,
Her young limbs
  Languished in the kitchen.   874

णोल्लेइ ऋणोल्लमणा ऋत्ता मं घरभरम्मि सऋलम्मि।
खणमेत्तं जह संझाए णवर ण व होइ वीसामो॥

A rigorous mother-in-law,
  The housework endless:
In the evening perhaps,
  But don't wait.   875

ठाणे ठाणे वलित्रा, वलणे वलणे सवेडसकुडुंगा।
ण गत्रो सि ऋम्ह गामं दित्ऋर! ण टिट्ठा तुए मुरला॥

> Stop lying, brother-in-law
>> You haven't seen my village,
> Nor the winding Murala
>> With many bends, many canebrakes.   876

महुएहि किं व वालत्र! हरसि णित्ऋम्बाहि जइ वि मे सित्ऋत्ऋं।
साहामि कस्स रण्णे दूरे गामो ऋहमेक्का॥

> Why mahua flowers, son?
>> Even if you grabbed my skirt,
> Who'd hear me in the forest?
>> The village's far, and I'm alone.   877

तत्थ वि होंति सहीऋो पुत्तलि! मा रुवसु जत्थ दिण्णा सि।
तत्थ वि णिउंजलीला, तत्थ वि गिरिवाहिणी गोदा॥

> Go, little one, and wipe your tears.
>> There are girl friends and reedstands
> In your husband's village,
>> And the Goda flowing through hills.   885

छप्पत्तित्रा वि खज्जइ णिप्पत्ते पुत्ति! एत्थ को दोसो?।
णित्रपुरिसे वि रमिज्जइ परपुरिसविवज्जिए गामे ॥

Sometimes, child,
    Eating scraps for dinner,
We have to make out with our husbands
    In manless villages.   887

त्रमुणित्रपरपुरिसुसहो जंपउ जं किं पि त्रण्णत्रो लोत्रो।
णित्रपुरिसेहि वि त्रगहे परपुरिसो च्चित्र रमामो ॥

Let faithful wives
    Say what they like,
I don't sleep with my husband
    Even when I do.   888

त्रव्वो! कालस्स गई, सो वि जुत्रा सरसकव्वदुल्ललित्रो।
पढइ परासरसहं त्रम्हे वि णित्रं पइं गमिमो ॥

Strange are time's ways.
    That young man given to poetry
Recites catechisms,
    And we to our husbands return.   892

अवराहसहस्साइं भरिमो हिअएण तम्मि अदिट्ठे।
दिट्ठम्मि उण, पित्तसही! एक्कं पि हु णं ण संभरिमो॥

When he's away
   His many infidelities
Come to mind:
   When I see him, none.   903

सोतुं सुहं ण लब्भइ, अव्वो! पेम्मस्स वंकविसमस्स।
दुग्घडिअमंचअस्स व खणे खणे पाअपडणेण॥

Love's like stretching out:
   The bedstead shaky, one leg
Falling off.   910

किं पि ण जंपसि कामं, भणिअं च करेसि तं तहा तुरिअं।
हिअअं रोसुव्वेअं ति तुज्झ विणअो च्चिअ कहेइ॥

Tacit, obedient,
   Solicitous,
Expressing her
   Wrath.   922

हंहो! किं व ण दिट्ठं हला! मए जीवित्रं धरन्तीए।
सो मं त्रणुणेइ पित्रो त्रहं पि त्रणुणिज्जिमि हत्रासा॥

Friend, what haven't
    I lived through?
He begged me to forgive him
    —And I did.   930

गाढालिंगणरभसुज्जुत्रम्मि दइए लहुं समोसरइ।
माणंसिणीएँ माणो पेल्लणभीत्रो व्व हित्रत्राहि॥

As he sprang forward
    To embrace her,
Her discreet pride
    Retreated.   934

त्रलित्रकुवित्रं पि कत्रमंतुत्रं व मं जेसु सुहत्र! त्रणुणेंतो।
ताण दित्रहाण हरणे रुत्रामि, ण उणो त्रहं कुवित्रा॥

Days when deceived
    By false anger,
You entreated me
    As if guilty:

O loved one,
    These tears
Are brought by
    Their passing.   941

तण्हा मे तुज्झ पित्रत्तणस्स, कह तं ति णोहि जाणामो।
दे सुहत्र! तुमं चित्र सिक्खवेसु जह दे पित्रा होमि॥

Always wanted
   To be your girl,
And didn't know how:
   Teach me.   948

फुप्फवइत्र म्हि बालत्र! मां चिवसु त्रदीहराउसो होसि।
त्रज्जं चेत्र मरिज्जउ मत्रच्छि! किं कालहरणेण॥

'Death comes early
   To those who touch
A woman in
   Her flowers.'

'Doe-eyed one,
   Let mine come
Now.'   950

केसा पाण्डुरछात्रा त्रसईसंगेण चम्म जज्जरित्रं।
चित्त तुहं सोहग्गं! गोदा दूइत्तणं कुणइँ॥

White-headed,
   Skin tattered by wantons,
But your luck still good:
   The Godavari's your go-between.   955

णिहुत्रररमणम्मि लोत्रणपहम्मि पडिए गुरुत्रणमज्झम्मि ।
सत्रलपरिहारहित्रत्रा वणगमणं चेत्र महइ वहू ॥

Catching sight of her lover
    Amidst her-in-laws,
The bride, renouncing all,
    Is sick for the paths of the forest.   987

AFTERWORD

The 207 Prākrit *gāthās* in this volume (*gāthās* are songs, but here the term refers to the metrical design of the verses) have been culled from an early anthology known chiefly by its Sanskrit name, the *Gāthāsaptaśatī* ('700 Verses in the *Gāthā* Form'). The anthology is known by various other Prākrit names, the most common ones being the *Sattasaī* ('The 700') and the *Gāhākoso* ('A Treasury of *Gāthās*').

The language of the *Gāthāsaptaśatī*, Maharashtri Prākrit, is classified by linguists as one of the Middle Indo-Aryan languages, all of which (save for Apabhraṃśa) are included under the generic name Prākrit. Middle Indo-Aryan includes dialects of inscriptions dating from the third century BC through the fourth century CE, as well as literary languages. The name Prākrit is derived from the Sanskrit word *prakṛti*, meaning 'making at first', 'original source'; 'nature'. Prākrit is the opposite of Sanskrit (from *saṃskṛti*, meaning 'well-made', 'refined'; 'cultured'). The traditional grammarians of the literary Prākrits argue that these languages are all derived from the Sanskrit language as codified by their predecessor, Pāṇini. But contemporary scholars employ the term Prākrit as it refers to the vernaculars, as opposed to Sanskrit, the language of so-called 'court' literature and of the educated and priestly classes. If we examine inscriptional evidence, it is clear that the Prākrits are not derivative. Prākrits were used for inscriptions as early as the third century BCE, where Sanskrit itself was not employed in inscriptions until as late as the first century CE.

There are many different varieties of literary Prākrits. The *gāthās* of this anthology were written in a Prākrit called Maharashtri ('from Maharashtra'). Its vocabulary is riddled with words which are definitely Dravidian in origin. Especially noticeable are kinship terms, which are prominent due to the fact that many of the verses are addressed to sisters (*akkā*), paternal aunts (*attā*) and mothers (*ammā*). This is strongly reminiscent of the poems of the Tamil Caṅkam anthology, the *Aiṅkuṟunūru*, as many of its verses are also addressed to its characters in this way.

According to the Prākrit grammarians, Maharashtri is the Prākrit *par excellence*. The very term Prākrit had become to them, in fact, a metonym for Maharashtri—when the term Prākrit was used in their discussions and analyses, it is clear that Maharashtri was usually what they meant. It is obvious that Prākrits such as Maharashtri must have been artificial, as they were different from the spoken languages contemporaneous with them and probably reflect vernaculars from some former time. So, in a sense, the *prakṛti* versus *saṃskṛti*/'nature' versus 'culture' dichotomy is not useful when we describe such a language. One could almost say that Maharashtri is a *saṃskṛta-prākṛt*, as it is itself a codified poetic language.

The Sanskrit poet Kālidāsa himself used Maharashtri in his dramas, perhaps out of some need for dramatic realism, thereby allowing the 'commoners' in his plays to speak a tongue which could adequately represent or suggest their own dialects. As far as we can tell, Kālidāsa was the first author to incorporate Maharashtri into a literary work, using it in the verses spoken by female characters in his dramas. His successors followed suit. George Hart has used this as the basis for dating the *Gāthāsaptaśatī*, placing it somewhere between Aśvaghoṣa and Kālidāsa (CE 200–450).

The metre of the Prākrit *gāthā* is what is known in Sanskrit prosody as *āryā* metre, of which sixteen varieties have been documented in Sanskrit itself. This scheme is more extensively elaborated in Prākrit *gāthās*, among which twenty-seven permutations are known to us. A *gāthā* consists of thirty *mātrās*, or 'syllabic instants', in the first line, which is subdivided into two *padas* ('feet'). The first *pada* consists of twelve *mātrās*; the second, of eighteen. The second line has twenty-seven *mātrās*, and is again divided into two *padas*; the first *pada* of this line also has twelve *mātrās*. The final *pada* follows with fifteen. In Prākrit versification, the metre is not based on the number of syllables in a line, as is the case in Sanskrit prosody. George Hart has indicated that it is, in fact, similar to Tamil metre in that it is based on the total *length* of syllables in a line. Hart uses this fact to suggest a historical relationship between Tamil and Prākrit metrical schemes, an entirely plausible suggestion.

Little is known about Hāla, the compiler of the *Gāthāsaptaśatī*. According to early commentaries, Hāla composed only forty-four of its verses. Hemacandra and family histories such as the *Deśīnāmamālā* list Hāla as a member of the Sātavāhana dynasty. One manuscript mentions Hāla as one of the lords of Kuntala-janapada, the southwest region of the former state of Hyderabad in modern-day Andhra Pradesh. A number of *Purāṇas* mention Hāla as the seventeenth Andhra king in a list of thirty.

According to this list, he reigned for only five years sometime during the first half of the first century CE.

Other well-known literary references to Hāla appear in the *Harṣacarita* of Bāṇa (circa CE 620) and in the *Kuvalayamala* of Uddyotana (circa CE 779): 'Hāla was pious if not religious. His partiality for Prākrits was often ridiculed.'

Since a full list of authors varies from commentary to commentary, it is difficult to draw any conclusions regarding definitive ascription. One commentary lists 261 other poets besides Hāla, including six or seven women poets, with ascriptions designated for 398 verses out of approximately 700. Bhūvanapāla's commentary lists 384 names.

Nearly every poem in this collection has love as its subject matter. When we think of love poetry from India, the first thing which comes to mind is the ornate descriptive verse contrived by poets writing under the patronage of the various royal courts of India's classical period. The poetry of Kālidāsa is, of course, the most accomplished verse of this genre. Its stateliness and elegance have fascinated readers, scholars and other poets (among them Goethe) for centuries. This poetry has given rise to the formation of conventions and rules which have served as guidelines for later works and held sway over Indian aesthetic thought for centuries.

However, Kālidāsa's idealized, perfect universe inhabited by lotus-eyed, moon-faced men and women was preceded by a world of a different sort—that of the Prākrit poets. Although lotus eyes and moonish faces do occasionally bloom within and illuminate the Prākrit terrain, the earthy description of love in all its many and sometimes 'indecent' forms is central to these verses. The *gāthās* are densely populated with misbehaving husbands and wives (as well as the sporadic errant child), as Verse 197 well illustrates:

> Tight lads in fields
>   A month in spring time,
> A cuss for a husband,
>   Liquor in the rack,
> And she young, free-hearted:
>   Asking her to be faithful
> Is asking her to die.

In these *gāthās*, the physical environment is as important as the physical act of love. The outside world is often described, often without the usual *dramatis personae*. The interplay between locale and characters is, as in Tamil *akam* poetry, a distinguishing feature of Prākrit verse. The effect of characters on locale is just as essential to the Prākrit aesthetic as the more familiar effect of locale on characters, a common conceit in the later and widely imitated Sanskrit poetry of Kālidāsa (see especially *Meghadūta* and *Ṛtusaṃhāra*). For example, Verse 218 describes the reaction of a flock of birds to a girl's loss of virginity on a riverbank (the trysting-place of choice in these poems). On the other hand, verses 58, 70 and 412 are exquisite examples of the effect of environment on characters.

If the *Gāthāsaptaśatī* is considered in the light of *rasa* theory, it becomes immediately evident that some of the verses exemplify *rasa*, but others are most definitely at odds with it. *Śṛṇgāra-rasa* ('the erotic mood or flavour') prevails, naturally, in both its modes; namely, union (*saṃbhoga*) and separation (*vipralambha*), as in the beauty and romance of Verse 132:

His form
    In my eyes,
His touch
    In my limbs,
His words
    In my ears,
His heart
    In my heart:
Now who's
    Separated?

And in the terse elegance of Verse 614:

Unaided by colour,
    Mere line locks them
    In deep embrace.

However, it is not only romance which has captured the fancy of Prākrit authors: the inelegant and downright awkward nature of physical love is also a favourite topic. In Verse 444, an inept and overeager lover is scolded through the conceit of indirect speech:

Before the white jasmine
    Could unfold, impetuous bee,
    You'd mangled it.

In Verse 483, we have an unusual motif, the frustration of a pregnant woman attempting to make love to her husband in *viparītarata* ('inverted intercourse').

Verse 104, a most exceptional verse in the entire collection, would certainly confound later *rasa* theoreticians by the way it mixes the erotic sentiment with that of terror (*bhayanaka-rasa*):

> Mournfully
> As if at the pyre
> Collecting
> Her loved one's relics
> The wanton
> Picked
> The last
> Mahua
> Blossoms

Poets and aestheticians of the late classical and medieval periods would consider such a mixture a defect (*doṣa*) and would therefore reject it.

The *gāthās* also play with the humorous aspects of love. Note dumbstruck lovers (162); the raucous teasing of girlfriends (145); a gorgeous girl who has entranced an entire village-full of men (593); or the lovely boast of one wife to another in verse 830, which is worth repeating here.

> Proud, aren't you, to display
> The beauty streaks
> Your husband's painted on your breasts?

> When I stood before mine,
> His hand lost all
> Control over the line.

Literary historians and orientalists seem to have made the general assumption that Prākrit languages and literatures are unsophisticated and vulgar, thereby perpetuating the Prākrit versus Sanskrit/'nature' versus 'culture' dichotomy. The *Gāthāsaptaśatī's* detractors and supporters alike have described it as derivative and sometimes as downright immoral. Arthur Berriedale Keith, in his now-classic reference work *Classical Sanskrit Literature*, rightly claims that Maharashtri Prākrit is 'far from being a true vernacular', but then argues that the *gāthās* are derived from the study of Sanskrit models. Keith has also demonstrated that the *Gāthāsaptaśatī* had a far-reaching influence on later authors and compilers of verse anthologies, and that it even 'found imitators in Sanskrit'. He continues to flatter the text, but his true pro-Sanskrit prejudices are clear: 'Govardhana's twelfth-century anthology, the *Āryāsaptaśatī*, is a collection of erotic verse arranged in alphabetical order. The work is inferior to Hāla's despite the superior beauty of the Sanskrit.'

When we turn to older poeticians, we find *gāthās* embedded in their Sanskrit *kāvyaśāstras* as examples of various rhetorical techniques. The ninth-century *Dhvanyāloka* of Ānandavardhana and the twelfth-century work of Mammata, *Kāvyaprakāśa*, are both replete with quotations from this anthology. These quotations enable us to contextualize many of the *gāthās* whose intentions might otherwise appear opaque, or, as in the example given below, as merely descriptive.

Verse 4 (not translated in the present collection) appears in the second chapter of the *Kāvyaprakāśa* as an example of suggestion (*vyañ-janā*, synonymous with *dhvani*):

> Look,
> a still, quiet crane
> glistens on a lotus leaf

like a conch shell lying
on a flawless emerald plate.

The vivid simile in this verse is part of a scenario: a woman and her lover are beside a riverbank and she spots a crane. She describes for the man a tranquil scene with an artful, well-matched simile. As modern readers, our first inclination would be to read this verse as a descriptive one and nothing more. But see what Mammata does with it: 'Here, by (the crane's) quietude, a state of confidence (is suggested), and by that (state of confidence), that the place is devoid of people. So, "This is a spot for trysting," says some woman to some man. Moreover, (the meaning) "You're lying, you didn't show up for our tryst" is suggested.' Mammata interprets this verse to mean that the woman is trying to seduce the man, and in the same breath accusing him of having missed an earlier rendezvous in that very spot.

The *gāthās* are used to demonstrate a wide variety of rhetorical techniques, but, as in the above example, they are primarily employed by the Sanskrit rhetoricians to explicate the technical functions of *dhvani*.

The author of the *Dhvanyāloka*, Ānandavardhana, understood 'resonance' or *dhvani* to be the very essence of poetry, and thought of it as the entire poetic process itself, with *rasa* as its second. All other poetic elements and techniques—*alaṃkāras* ('figures'), *guṇas*, ('qualities') and so on are subordinate to *dhvani* and *rasa*. Ānandavardhana was himself a Prākrit poet, and in his *Dhvanyāloka* the *gāthā* poems illustrate a number of his most important arguments.

For example, Ānandavardhana employs the *gāthās* as illustrations of the *dhvani* that is *svataḥ sambhavī*, or '*dhvani* that occurs naturally', a division of *arthaśakitmūladhvani*, '*dhvani* having its base in the power of sense'.

Ānandavardhana says in *Dhvanyāloka* II.24 that 'one meaning which suggests another is . . . two-fold: it either exists only in ornate expression or it occurs naturally'. He further explains that the first exists only in the ornate expression of the poet himself or in that of a character created by him. The second actually exists in the real world, and does not owe its existence to the ornaments of poetic expression. Then, as an example of the latter, which we would not be hard-pressed to understand as 'realism', he cites Verse 173 (not translated in the present collection), a wonderful picture of 'naturally occurring' female rivalry:

> Hanging peacock feathers
> from her ears,
> the hunter's wife struts
> before all her pearl-clad rivals.

It is evident therefore that Hāla's *Gāthāsaptaśatī* had captured both the imagination and the taste of medieval Sanskrit rhetoricians. We can go one step further and examine the *gāthās* in relation to other bodies of classical Indian poetry: the 'court poetry' of the Sanskrit tradition and the Tamil poetry of the Caṅkam age.

Let us look at three poems, one each from Sanskrit, Tamil and Maharashtri. They contain within them an object—a parrot. Let us chase this object through several centuries of poetry to see what it can tell us about changes and differences in poetics. The first poem is number 616 from the *Subhāṣitaratnakośa*, a Sanskrit anthology compiled by the Buddhist scholar Vidyākara sometime during the late eleventh or early twelfth century CE. The poem has no ascribed author. The verse forms part of a section titled 'the evidence of consummation' (*samāptanidhuvancih-navrajyā*; Ingalls: 1965). The second poem, by Kapilar, is from the *Aiṅkuṟunūru* ('The Short 500'), a Tamil anthology from the earliest layers of the Caṅkam period. This verse is one of ten on parrots from a section of the work entitled *Kiḷḷaip pattu* ('Parrot Decad'). The decad is, in turn, a part of a hundred-verse section entirely composed by Kapilar, on 'love in union', the *kuṟiñci* theme. The last verse is number 75 from the *Gāthāsaptaśatī* (not translated in the present collection).

I will present the poems first in transliteration, then in translation:

Subhāṣitaratnakośa 616

uṣasi gurusamakṣaṃ lajjamānā mṛgākṣi ratirutamanuk-
    artuṃ rājakīre pravṛtte
tirayati śīśulī lānartanacchadmatālapracalavalayamālāsp-
    hālakolāhalena

> At daybreak
> when the parrot
> was bent on mimicking
> her cries of passion
> in front of her elders
> the girl
> embarrassed
> doe-eyed
> covered it up
> by jangling
> her stacks of bangles
> clapping
> as if to make
> the children dance in play

Aiṅkuṟunūru 281

veḷḷa varampin ūli pōkiyum
kiḷḷai vāḷiya palavē ōḷḷilai
irumpal kūntar koticci
peruntōṭ kāval kāṭṭi yavvē.

May parrots outlive
the flood at the end of time!

They've caused this clatter
made by the long arms
of the woman
with the thick black hair
and many gleaming jewels.

Gāthāsaptaśatī 75

ua pommarāa-maragga-saṃvaliā ṇaha-alāo oarai
ṇaha-siri-kaṇṭha-bohaṭṭha vva kaṇṭhiā kīra-riñcholī

Look,
coral and emeralds mixed
fall from heaven
like a necklace unstrung
from the throat of the sky-goddess:

a line of parrots!

When we look at these three love poems, each one as
sophisticated as the other, it is clear that the authors have
chosen to use the parrot in an iconic way.

The Sanskrit verse is an erotic sketch, an almost painterly
rendering. The verse is a bi-dimensional sexual vignette. In
the original Sanskrit, it is also heavily embellished—
encrusted with elaborate rhetorical ornamentation—a piece

of high Sanskrit rococo. The ornaments are particularly apparent in the onomatopoeia in the long compound word in the second line. Nothing is left to the imagination and all possible elements are incorporated—time, the parrot and the function of the parrot, bedroom moans, judgemental in-laws, the girl, her eyes and her embarrassment, and the din of her feint. Everything is *in praesentia*; the poem moves in a linear fashion and its meaning is conveyed primarily through its syntax.

The eroticism of the Tamil verse from the *Aiṅkuṟunūru* is less apparent. Again, the parrot is a cause. The theme of the verse is called 'the guarding of the millet' (*puṉaṉkāval*) in Tamil poetics. The male speaker of the poem is praising the parrots because their raids on the outlying millet fields bring the young women outside. The women rush to the fields with sticks and clappers to frighten off the plundering birds. These fields are trysting places and the verse speaks of a happy memory, a certain girl with abundant hair and glittering jewellery. The poem is spare, unlike the Sanskrit verse. Its complexity lies in its semantics. The parrot here is not simply a causal element but a 'paradigmatic' one as well; its presence in the verse alludes to certain erotic paradigms of which it is a part, moving the poem to a third dimension of resonance, fetching a memory of love and inciting a renewed longing.

That the Prākrit poem is an erotic verse may not at all be apparent to a fresh reader. It strikes us at first as a beautiful descriptive verse. Like Verse 4, cited earlier, it seems to have a simile and nothing more. And yet, like Verse 4, this too is erotic not due to the presence of specifically erotic elements, but due to the absence of these very elements. The eroticism is dependent on both *paradigmatic resonance* (*dhvani* in its purest sense) and on *poetic diction*. In this verse, a male is speaking to a woman whom he wants to seduce. According to two modern Hindi commentaries, the mere mention of parrots at all is an allusion to sexual intercourse. The parrots' descent from the sky to the trees and downwards brings the girl's eye from the sky to the ground. The ground beneath the trees is where trysts take place in Prākrit poems. The unstrung necklace suggests the unravelling of her virginity, or perhaps her braid. There is promiscuity in the fall of a parrot.

In both the Tamil verse and the *gāthā*, the varying degrees of absence of explicit erotic elements lead the reader towards a certain type of literary participation. The Sanskrit verse asks us to admire it. It is a closed system. Everything in it is domestic as well as domesticated—the parrot is a caged pet as is the house-bound wife, and there is no mention of the world outside. The Tamil poem asks us to praise parrots, to share in a memory, and perhaps to help create a collective longing. But the Prākrit verse seduces us right along with the woman to whom it is addressed. With its very first word, *ua*, it invites us to 'look' from the sky to the ground and to enter into participation with it.

A major and obvious feature of a Prākrit *gāthā* is its sheer brevity. A *gāthā* is defined and shaped by certain metrical requirements and by its erotic subject matter. A *gāthā*, to be a *gāthā*, had to compress a lot of meaning into a very brief poem. The *gāthās* became encoded for paradigmatic messages with the use of allusion and *double entendre*. The *gāthās* are generally free of rhetorical embellishments and the vocabulary is refreshingly simple, making these poems clean, sleek transmitters of meaning through *dhvani*. *Dhvani* is both the means and the end of the Prākrit poetry. The *gāthās* are poetry refined in the best of crucibles, distilling complexity, meaning and delight in their purest, simplest forms.

Martha Ann Selby
University of Chicago
1997

Sources Cited

Aiṅkuṟunūṟu. Ettuttokaiyul Mūṉrāvatākiya Aiṅkuṟunūṟu Mūlamum Palaiyav Uraiyum. Edited by Doctor U. Vē. Cāminataiyar. Ceṉṉai: Ṭākṭar U. Vē. Cāminataiyar Nūl Nilaiyam, 1980.

Ānandavardhana. *Dhvanyāloka of Anandavardhana.* Critically edited with introduction, English translation, and notes by K. Krishnamoorthy. Dharwar: Karnatak University, 1974.

Hāla. *Gāthāsaptaśatī.* Edited with introduction and Hindi commentary by Paramānanda Śāstrī. Meerut: Prakāśan Pratiṣṭhān, 1965.

_____ *Gāthāsaptaśatī.* Edited with the 'Prakāśa' Hindi commentary by Jagannātha Pāṭhaka. Vārāṇasī: Chowkhamba Sanskrit Series Office, 1969.

_____ *The Prākrit Gāthā-Saptaśatī Compiled by Śatavāhana King Hāla.* Edited with introduction and English translation by Radhagovinda Basak. Calcutta: The Asiatic Society, 1971.

Hart, George L. III. *The Poems of Ancient Tamil: Their Milieu and their Sanskrit Counterparts.* Berkeley: University of California Press, 1975.

Keith, Arthur Berriedale. *Classical Sanskrit Literature* (sixth edition). New Delhi: Y.M.C.A. Publishing House, 1966.

Ingalls, Daniel H.H. *An Anthology of Sanskrit Court Poetry.* Cambridge: Harvard University Press, 1965.

Krishnamoorthy, K. *Essays in Sanskrit Criticism.* Dharwar: Karnatak University, 1964.

Mammaṭa. *Kāvyaprakāsa*. With the commentary 'Bālabodhinī' by Vamanacarya Ramabhatta Jhalakikar. Edited by Raghunath Damodar Karmarkar. Poona: Bhandarkar Oriental Research Institute, 1965.

The Subhāṣitaratnakośa. Compiled by Vidyākara. Edited by D.D. Kosambi and V.V. Gokhale with an introduction by D.D. Kosambi. Cambridge: Harvard University Press, 1957.

NOTES TO THE POEMS

Unlike its Tamil cousin, the Prākrit *gāthā* does not have a colophon to give the poem's speaker ('What Her Girl Friend Said') and set the scene (*her lover within earshot, behind a fence*). The commentaries on the *Gāthāsaptaśatī* sometimes disagree on these points, and I have in the notes below relied chiefly on Gaṅgādhara's sixteenth-century (?) work to identify the voice and, more interestingly, the intention behind it.

The poems are numbered according to Albrecht Weber's *Das Saptaçatakam des Hāla* (Leipzig, 1881), and the references are to the numbers of the poems. The translations up to Poem 701 were made from Mathuranath Sastri's edition, and thereafter from S.A. Jogalekar's. Both editions follow Weber's text.

Poem 2. This introductory *gāthā* is one of approximately eighty-two poems from the *Gāthāsaptaśatī* in Jayavallabh's *Vajjālaggaṃ* (Patwardhan 1969), a Prākrit anthology compiled between the eighth and fourteenth centuries.

Poem 9. The first of several poems on trysting-places (*saṃketa-sthāna*). The heroine is consoled by her girl friend who shows her an alternative rendezvous, a hemp yard yellow with flowers; compare 693. Some others in this genre are 103, 104, 110, 295, 402, 550, 628, 676, 769 and 874. For commentatorial approaches to these and other rendezvous poems, see Dundas (1985).

Poem 11. The scene at her feet reminds the woman of a coital position—'the postilion position' as Flaubert called it—and hence the laughter (Gaṅgādhara).

Poem 24. Any wife to any husband, sitting beside her out of a sense of duty.

Poem 30. The hero, a poor wife-ridden man, and knowing no better, misses out on sweeter opportunities.

neem: *Azadirachta indica*; evergreen tree of India and Malaysia; its leaves and bark are bitter, and insects generally leave it alone.

Poem 36. A rare example of a faithful wife who, despite all odds, keeps to the straight and narrow.

Poem 43. mother: Prākrit *mae*, used in the sense of an older woman.

Poem 49. The speaker is a *swayaṃdūtī*, a woman who is her own go-between. See also 335, 550 and 669.

Poem 52. According to Mathuranath Sastri, the heroine, having chided her man for being a poor lover, takes his position and is soon exhausted. For once it gives him something to talk about.

For a nice perspective on *viparītarata* or 'contrary intercourse', see Ingalls (1965: Intr. 19, par. 10). Other verses on this variation are 391, 483 and 656.

Poem 56. A bawd indicates to a customer that no matter how inexpert the man, her girl is not one to complain (Gaṅgādhara).

sirissa: *Albizzia lebbek*; a large deciduous tree with an umbrella-shaped crown and fragrant, delicate white flowers. The field guides to Indian trees sometimes quote a few lines of Sanskrit poetry in their entry on the sirissa.

Poem 58. This ambiguous poem is 374 in the *Vajjālaggaṃ*, where it appears in 'The Section on Separation'; for a detailed note, see Patwardhan (1969: 479–80).

Poem 70. 'What Her Girl Friend Said' to a *prôshitabhatṛika* (a woman whose husband is abroad); for a parallel Caṅkam poem and its discussion, see Ramanujan (1985: 240).

new clouds: a sign of the first rains and the coming monsoon, the season of lovemaking. See also 386.

Another consolatory poem, but spoken, say, a month later,

is 729. For a glimpse of the husband on the road, see 696; and on arrival, 707.

Poem 103. See note on Poem 9. According to Gaṅgādhara, a loose woman (*kulaṭā*), who wants to be made love to, intends the speech not for the trysting-tree but her ardent lover.

mahua: *Bassia latifolia*; a deciduous medium-sized tree common throughout the Indian plains and in the rocky hill-regions of the Deccan. Its musk-scented creamy flowers that fall at night are gathered at dawn and can be added to cooking or fermented and distilled to make a liquor similar to gin.

Poem 104. See note on Poem 9.

Poem 107. She presumably wants to catch the man's attention.

Poem 110. See note on Poem 9. Said to her aunt, her lover within earshot. Having made the appointment, he failed to come, whereas she, under pretext of fetching water from the pond before it was muddied, kept the early tryst (Gaṅgādhara).

Perhaps the best gloss on the poem is Pound's note to Rihaku's 'The Jewel Stairs' Grievance'. The first two lines suggest a cloudless sky, 'therefore he has no excuse on account of weather' (Pound 1953: 194); the last two that despite perfect conditions there could be no lovemaking. 'The poem is especially prized because she utters no direct reproach' (Pound 1953: 194).

However, *Dhvanyāloka* II.31 quotes it as an example of a poem in which 'the expressed is more important than the implied' (Krishnamoorthy 1982: 103).

Poem 121. Were he alive, the brave hunter would not have allowed the dangerous *must* elephant to come near the *Karañja* (Jogalekar). His wife has, in Umberto Eco's words, recognized 'the evidence through which the world speaks to us like a great book' (Eco 1984: 23).

Karañja: *Pongamia pinnate*; this modest-sized evergreen tree is a native of the Western Ghats where it is found chiefly along the banks of streams and near coastal regions; its seed and roots are used in indigenous medicine.

Poem 132. A woman, whose husband is abroad, to a wicked go-between come on a mission (Gaṅgādhara).

Poem 136. A bawd to a miserly customer, in the hope of making him part with a little more money (Gaṅgādhara).

Poem 138. A go-between to the young hero, advising him to make up with the ingénue before it is too late (Gaṅgādhara).

Poem 161. 'These girls [at a well] offered the traveller cool water, and sometimes more than that' (Ingalls 1965: Intr. 9, par. 5).

Poem 162. The bhikshu is the heroine's lover visiting her in disguise; the speaker is her co-wife addressing their mother-in-law who wants to know what keeps her at the door (Gaṅgādhara). Other commentators, however, call it a poem of love at first sight.

Poem 200. The bite indicates that the woman's lying-in period is over and, her strength back, she is once again ready for lovemaking; the smile indicates that it is her tooth-mark—and not the child's—on the berry (Gaṅgādhara).

Poem 205. A go-between to the hero, to suggest that his fear likewise is based on a misapprehension (Gaṅgādhara).

Poem 231. The heroine to her lover's friend (Gaṅgādhara).

Poem 238. The heroine to her lover, of late paying more attention to his young wife than to her (Gaṅgādhara).

Poem 239. 'Child-bearing women who never wanted to conceive, and who, when they finally die after their eighth child, had the gestures and the lightness of young girls looking forward to love' (Rilke 1984: 128).

Poem 249. For a prolix imitation, see Ingalls (1965: Poem 826).

Poem 258. A procuress on her girl's strong point? Or, one *flâneur* to another?

Poem 273. In her lover's absence, the heroine becomes disinterested in her appearance and wears her hair in one plait; she says this to him when he returns.

Poem 274. The lady of situations to a hesitant young man.

Poem 287. The heroine, who feels neglected because her lover does not bring her gifts, being advised on honest love by a go-between (Gaṅgādhara); 'The animals have little, but that little is useful and true' (Linscott 1957: 12).

The *Alaṃkārakaustubha* refers to the poem as an example of *aprastutapraśaṃsā*, 'a figure in which the real but implicit subject matter is obliquely referred to by means of an explicit, but apparently irrelevant, subject which, however, stands in a specific relationship to the former (Gerow 1971: 111).

Poem 291. The woman wants to show her armpit and breasts (Gaṅgādhara).

Poem 295. See note on Poem 9.

Poem 332. A go-between to the hero, to indicate she knows what is going on (Gaṅgādhara).

Poem 335. See note on Poem 49. The night is dark, so the neighbour can enter her house unnoticed; her husband has just left, so they have some time before he returns (Gaṅgādhara).

Jogalekar, who invents a Marathi and English title for each poem, calls this one 'Invitation'.

Poem 351. 'I have a fornication coming up that worries me considerably, and which I mustn't shirk, although I want to make it chaste—that is, literary, without gross details or lascivious images: the carnality must be in the emotion' (Steegmuller 1981: 191).

Poem 355. An old procuress, teasing someone on his way to the trysting-place (Gaṅgādhara).

Poem 372. An old woman remembers the unorthodox ways of her youth. The stone is a Gaṇeśa idol; it is now in worship but has seen better days.

Poem 379. The implication is that they have spent the night together and she will not see him again (Gaṅgādhara).

Poem 386. See note on Poem 70.

Poem 391. The heroine, desirous of 'contrary intercourse' (see note on Poem 52), to her lover (Gaṅgādhara).

Poem 396. An instance of the gallows humour of homebound travellers; for the woman's response to the mango buds, see Poem 499.

Poem 402. See note on Poem 9. The heroine indicates to her lover, or a go-between to an *abhisārikā* (a woman on her way to meet her lover), that the barley field is no longer safe for the tryst (Gaṅgādhara). The suggested meaning could also be its opposite. The heroine spreads the falsehood about the sow so as to scare others from approaching the field; the signal to her lover is that he can now go there without fear (Jogalekar).

Poem 412. night jasmine: *Nyctanthes arbor tristis*; a shrub or small tree of southern Asia, with fragrant night-blooming—and night-dying—flowers (Skt. *sephālī*).

Poem 414. If this is read as a rendezvous poem, see also Poem 628.

Poem 434. The heroine to her lover, suggesting he reach the trysting-place; or, an old courtesan's riposte to a pander, to tell him she is not the only one turning grey (Gaṅgādhara).

káns: Saccharum spontaneum; a widely distributed coarse grass, bearing a white tuft-like panicle; its period of inflorescence is from mid-September to February. It is commonly seen on mud banks of paddy fields and along banks of rivers.

Poem 442. By giving the bee's example, a shrewd woman teaches a sexual position to a man keen to make love to a nonaged girl; or, a messenger to a young bride, indicating that her husband is adept in the art of love and will not cause her pain (Gaṅgādhara).

Poem 483. See note on Poem 52.

Poem 499. The evil in the mango tree is its buds, proclaiming spring to a woman whose traveller-husband is abroad. Jogalekar's title for it is 'How Do You Do?'

For the response of two travellers to the buds, see 396.

Poem 550. See notes on poems 9 and 49.

Poem 564. By drawing his attention to the rain, the heroine indicates to her lover that their lovemaking need not be rushed through since no one is now likely to disturb them (Gaṅgādhara).

Poem 599. If the same poem can exist originally in two languages, then this one does. The English original is by Tony Harrison:

I bought three *Players* tins
of groundnuts with green mould
just to touch your hand
counting coppers into mine.

(Harrison 1984: 35)

Poem 628. See notes on Poems 9 and 414.

Poem 636. Pulinda: a tribe of wild mountaineers.

Poem 656. See note on Poem 52.

Poem 662. A go-between to an *abhisārikā*, to indicate that night is about to fall and she must hasten to the tryst (Gaṅgādhara).

Poem 664. She feeds the dog when her lover is around, and when her husband is around, she starves it (Pītāmbar).

Poem 669. See note on Poem 49. *Dhvanyāloka* I.4 quotes this poem—and makes it famous—as an example of one kind of implicit meaning: 'Sometimes, though the explicit meaning is of the nature of a prohibition, the implicit will be of the nature of a positive proposal' (Krishnamoorthy 1982: 9).

A variation of this is in Ingalls (1965: Poem 812).

Poem 676. See note on Poem 9. The daughter-in-law returns from a tryst in a bamboo grove, and, should she point a finger at her, warns her mother-in-law that her back too has signs not less telltale.

Poem 684. The image recurs in Thomas Hardy:

The Roman road runs straight and bare
As the pale parting-line in hair
Across the heath.

(Hardy 1979: 264)

Poem 693. See note on Poem 9.

Poem 696. See note on Poem 70.

Poem 707. See note on Poem 70.

Poem 718. For more poems on the go-between's treachery and 'The Lady's Expression of Anger', see Ingalls (1965: Sec. 25).

Poem 729. See note on Poem 70.

Poem 746. Sea-going vessels carried a crow on board to help sailors search for land; also see Patwardhan (1969: 474).

Poem 769. See note on Poem 9.

Poem 825. mother: see note on Poem 43.

Poem 874. See note on Poem 9. The woman's lover has reached the trysting-place, his arrival indicated by the birds' flutter, whereas she, delayed perhaps by her mother-in-law's presence, is unable to join him.

Poem 876. Murala: a river in the extreme southwest of India.

Poem 888. The complications of this fantasy are brought out in a conversation between Querry and Marie Ryeker in *A Burnt-Out Case*:

> 'What on earth are you talking about now?'
> 'I didn't want him. The only way I could manage was to shut my eyes and think it was you.'
> 'I suppose I ought to thank you,' Querry said, 'for the compliment.'
> 'It was then that the baby must have started. So you see it wasn't a lie that I told them.'
> 'Not a lie?'
> 'Only a half-lie. If I hadn't thought all the time of you, I'd have been all dried up and babies don't come so easily then, do they? So in a way it is your child.'
>
> (Greene 1961: 236)

Poem 892. A similar poem of resignation reaches us also through 'The Love Poems of the VIth Dalai Lama':

> Why does this pretty boy from Kong-po
> buzz like a trapped bee?
> He has been my bed-mate for three days
> and now thinks only of god . . .
>
> (Whigham 1969: 18)

Poem 955. According to Jogalekar, the medium, a leaf-cup filled with flowers carried downstream by the river-as-go-between, is the message.

Two thousand years later Ruben Dario, as if he had read the old man's thoughts, wrote:

> But in spite of stubborn time,
> My thirst for love persists;
> I approach the garden's roses,
> My hair a greying mist.

(Monegal and Reid 1981: 245, n. 3)

REFERENCES

Prākrit Sources

Das Saptaçatakam des Hāla. 1881. Edited by Albrecht Weber. Leipzig: F.A. Brockhaus.

Gāthāsaptaśatī, 1911. With a commentary by Gaṅgādhara, edited by Durgaprasad and Pansikar. 2nd ed. Kavyamālā Series. Bombay: Nirnaya Sagar Press.

—— 1933. Edited with a Sanskrit commentary by Mathuranath Sastri. 3rd ed. Bombay: Nirnaya Sagar Press.

Hāla Sātavāhanācī Gāthāsaptaśatī. 1956. Edited with a Marathi commentary by S.A. Jogalekar. Pune: Prasad Prakashan.

Hāritāmrapītāmbara's Gāthāsaptaśatī prakāśikā. 1942. Edition (IV–VII *satakas*) with Pītāmbara's commentary, edited by Jagdish Lal. Lahore: n.p.

Other Works

Dundas, Paul. 1985. *The Sattasaī and its Commentators*. Torino: Publicazioni di Indologica Taurinensia.

Eco, Umberto. 1984. *The Name of the Rose*, tr. William Weaver. London: Pan Books.

Gerow, Edwin. 1971. *A Glossary of Indian Figures of Speech*. The Hague: Mouton.

Greene, Graham. 1961. *A Burnt-Out Case*. London: William Heinemann.

Hardy, Thomas. 1979. *The Complete Poems*, ed. James Gibson. London: Macmillan.

Harrison, Tony. 1984. *Selected Poems*. Harmondsworth: Penguin Books.

Ingalls, Daniel H.H. 1965. *An Anthology of Sanskrit Court Poetry*. Cambridge: Harvard University Press.

Krishnamoorthy, K. 1982. *Dhvanyāloka of Anandavardhan*. Edition with English translation. 2nd ed. Delhi: Motilal Banarsidass.

Linscott, Robert N., ed. 1957. *The Notebooks of Leonardo da Vinci*. New York: Modern Library.

Monegal, Emir Rodriguez and Alastair Reid, eds. 1981. *Borges: A Reader*. New York: E.P. Dutton.

Patwardhan, M.V. 1969. *Jayavallabh's Vajjālaggaṃ*. Edited with English translation and notes. Prakrit Text Series. Ahmedabad: Prakrit Text Society.

Pound, Ezra. 1953. *The Translations of Ezra Pound*. London: Faber and Faber.

Ramanujan, A.K. 1985. *Poems of Love and War*. Delhi: Oxford University Press.

Rilke, Rainer Maria. 1984. *The Notebook of Malte Laurids Brigge*, tr. by John Linton. 1st ed. 1930; rpt. Oxford. Oxford University Press.

Steegmuller, Francis, ed. 1981. *The Letters of Gustave Flaubert: 1830–1857*. London: Faber and Faber.

Whigham, Peter. 1969. *The Blue Winged Bee*. London: Anvil Press Poetry.